Mobile Security: How to Secure, Privatize, and Recover Your Devices

Keep your data secure on the go

Tim Speed

Darla Nykamp

Mari Heiser

Joseph Anderson

Jaya Nampalli

BIRMINGHAM - MUMBAI

Mobile Security: How to Secure, Privatize, and Recover Your Devices

First published: September 2013

Production Reference: 1300813

Published by Packt Publishing Ltd.
Livery Place
35 Livery Street
Birmingham B3 2PB, UK.

ISBN 978-1-84969-360-8

www.packtpub.com

Cover Image by Amit Gajera (86amitpixs@gmail.com)

Credits

Authors
Tim Speed

Darla Nykamp

Mari Heiser

Joseph Anderson

Jaya Nampalli

Reviewers
Michael Clarkson

Jason Slater

Acquisition Editor
Martin Bell

Lead Technical Editor
Mayur Hule

Technical Editors
Jalasha D'costa

Larissa Pinto

Amit Ramadas

Project Coordinator
Anugya Khurana

Proofreader
Maria Gould

Indexer
Mariammal Chettiyar

Graphics
Abhinash Sahu

Production Coordinator
Nilesh R. Mohite

Cover Work
Nilesh R. Mohite

Foreword

Today, nearly every individual uses some kind of intelligent mobile device and for you, the end user, it is important to understand the risks inherent in using these devices. The benefit is obvious, but keeping yourself and your family safe in this mobile world is more essential than ever. *Mobile Security: How to Secure, Privatize, and Recover Your Devices* will be invaluable to those who want to know how to protect themselves in this new mobile world. The authors explain how to protect your device, as well as the actions you should take in the event that your personal information or device is compromised. This book is intended as a guide; it has thus been organized for convenient reference in addressing the issues and challenges inherent in navigating the new mobile world.

Contained within this book is a list of available mobile devices and their uses. Also, features such as Facebook, LinkedIn, Connection, Groupon, and others are discussed with regards to their potential for exposing users to risk. Mobile banking and purchases are also included in this discussion. Exposure of our financial information to potential hackers should be of major concern to those that participate in these activities. On a related note, Cloud computing is addressed and defined, with particular attention paid to the risks and security weaknesses of this increasingly important popular technology.

The inclusion of Mobile Device Management (MDM) is significant because of the increasing number of personal devices, which are used at work. When your personal device connects to a company's trusted network, your employer's security measures must be put into effect. These security measures go far beyond simply creating new passwords. One issue identified and discussed in this book is personally downloaded programs. These applications may contain viruses, which may therefore place your employer's proprietary information at risk. This handbook will help you to understand how to protect yourself and your employer.

We all interact with our world using a variety of mobile devices. To verify our identification, we are forced to enter personal information. This information is now held by numerous sites, banks, social media, mobile storefronts, cell phone carriers, and many more. This book explains what these sites do with your information and the control you, as an individual, have. Everyone needs to understand the privacy and customer information polices of any business to which they provide their personal information.

The threats and challenges, which users in the mobile world may encounter, are presented in a detailed and easy-to-understand format. This book provides a list of actions the users can take to protect themselves, such as how to strengthen passwords and techniques for encrypting personal data. The possibility that a hacker is able to circumvent such preventative measures is also addressed. You as an end user are not helpless against hackers. A comprehensive list of steps to take in case a hacker is successful is included. There is also a guide on how to inform law enforcement, and what to expect afterwards.

Protecting your devices is, however, the primary focus of this book. Therefore, a discussion of insurance and third-party tools that can keep your device and information safe is included. Monitoring your credit through services such as Lifelock is also covered. As part of this discussion, this handbook also covers in detail the steps you can take to remove your private information from websites such as Facebook or Twitter.

The section on future scenarios is useful and timely, as it discusses the trajectory of mobile technology and security. Some of the options mentioned are already available to the general public; those that are not yet publicly available may be in the very near future. Our society is moving away from the brick-and-mortar consumer world of yesterday. Paper money is slowly going the path of paper checks. Our information will have to be available in this virtual society and therefore, the value of such information will only increase. Correspondingly, it is more essential than ever that we learn how to better protect ourselves; this book provides techniques tailored for this new and more challenging environment.

Chapter 8, Getting Your Life Back After You've Been Hacked, is a template where the reader can enter the information they will need in case their information is in danger of being compromised. It is a useful tool, as reacting in a timely manner is essential. I recommend you take time to fill it out.

Steve Robinson

VP of Development, Product Management and Strategy,
IBM Security Systems Division

About the Authors

Tim Speed is an IBM Senior Certified Systems Architect with IBM Software Services for Collaboration. In that capacity, he is responsible for designing, implementing, and supporting various engagements with IBM customers. Tim has been an IBM employee for over 18 years in a variety of networking, technical, hardware, and software support and consulting positions. He has been working with Lotus Notes for over 20 years, focusing on administration roles and infrastructure. He also has international experience with working on infrastructure engagements in Spain, The Bahamas, Japan, Hong Kong, Singapore, Malaysia, the UK, and Indonesia.

A very special acknowledgment to the Commissioner of Police, Ellison Greenslade, of The Royal Bahamas Police Force.

Also, thanks to the IBM management team that provided approval to publish this book: Walter L Berthelsen, Jack Shoemaker, Luis Pineda, Mark Guerinot, and thanks to our sponsor, Steve Robinson. Thanks to Steve Robinson for writing the foreword for this book. Thanks to the Packt Publishing team for their help and support, specially Anugya Khurana and Martin Bell. Special thanks to Victor Ross for reviewing many of my books. Thanks to Vijay Dheap for your comments and feedback on this book.

Also I thank my wife, Linda Speed, and son, Johnathon Speed, for helping me with the book and providing some of the editing throughout the various chapters. Next, I want to thank my mother, Lillian Speed, for teaching me to "think big". Thanks to Jo Stinebaugh; also thanks to all the co-authors—you all did a great job!

Other acknowledgments include: Katherine and Sean Mullins, Chris Cotton, Steven Stansel, Mark Steinborn, Jason Erickson, John Allessio, Tony Higham, Brad Schauf, Scott Souder, David Byrd, Jeff Pinkston, David Bell, Gary Wood, Robert Thietje, Jessie and Wanda Rodgers, Marlene Botter, Mike Dudding, Stephen Cooke, Dr Seshagiri Rao, Jose Burbano, Alistair Rennie, Amanda Vance, Barry Rosen, Charles K. DeLone, Don Bunch, Ed Speed, Matthew Speed, Chuck Stauber, David R. Hinkle, Doug Parham, Frederic Dahm, Gary Ernst, William and Sherry Destache, Gary Desmarais, Hissan C Waheed, Jay Cousineau, Jayasree Nampalli, Dr. John Lamb, and special thanks to "John Norton"; also thanks to: Kevin Lynch, Marc Galeazza, Marco M Noel, Steve Matrullo, Steven J Amadril, Terry Fouchey, Dellareece Ferguson, Kimbler Smith, Kevin Roberts, Shona Woods, Jevone Ferguson, Karoldann Darville, Harry Dolce, Zhivago Dames, Anthony DiDonato, Tim Cardwell, Barry Heinz, Cynthia L. Oehmig, Scot Bentley, Brian C Erle, Peter Volkmar, Claude Roy, David Saunders, Dieter Poetzschke, Hunter Medney, David and Dana Jea, Joe Christopher, Dennis Anderson, John J Johnson, William Nunez, Kevin Mills, Kevin Pare, Kevin Peake, Melanie Skinner, Pam Fryer, Rahul Vyas, Robert McDonald, Steven Kramer, and Jim and Nadia Kilnoski, Clark and Stephanie Oberly, and Tony Cusato.

Darla Nykamp is an Internal Auditor with IBM, joining the company in 1996 after more than a decade in the IT industry. She has focused on software design and development, security policy design and implementation, business controls and compliance, and served as IBM's first Global Privacy Delivery Leader.

In her spare time, Darla earned a Doctorate of Law, a Master's degree in International Business Management, a Bachelor's degree in Computer Science, and certifications in security and privacy professions.

Deep thanks to my loving family and friends whose support and encouragement were always available.

Thanks also to my sweet basset hound, Princess, who sacrificed walks to allow me to finish "just one more page".

Mari Heiser is an IBM and Open Group Master Certified Architect with over 20 years of architecture, governance, risk, compliance, and technical management experience in networks and web technologies, specializing in security, compliance, and Service Oriented Architecture (SOA). Mari is also an expert in Identity and Access Management, Cloud, Security Analytics, and leads the IBM internal Information Security Community of Practice for the Americas. Mari's industry-specific experience has been concentrated in banking, manufacturing, distribution, bio-tech, education, and aerospace industries.

Thanks to Packt Publishing for their support and editing over this process.

My sincere thanks to Jim for his patience while I worked late nights, and to Heather for keeping me grounded and on the right path.

Joseph Anderson is an IBM Certified Managing Consultant from the IBM Collaboration Solutions Software Team. Joseph has worked with IBM Notes/ Domino, IBM Connections, IBM Sametime, IBM WebSphere Portal, and IBM Quickr since the early 1990s, primarily as a consultant. He is currently responsible for managing complex Customer Engagements focusing on assisting customers with the development, licensing, and deployment of complex environments. Prior to working in the consulting industry, Joseph worked in the legal industry as a Director of Operations, where he leveraged his Master's of Science in Legal Administration from the University of Denver College of Law. Joseph is the co-author of two books: *IBM Lotus Notes and Domino 8.5.3: Upgrader's Guide* by *Packt Publishing* and *Lotus Notes Domino 8: Upgrader's Guide* by *Packt Publishing*. Additionally, Joseph was a Technical Reviewer for *IBM Lotus Notes 8.5.3 How-to* by *Packt Publishing*.

I would like to dedicate my efforts towards this book to Lisa, my loving wife and best friend, and to my father, Gary, who without knowing it led me to technology and ultimately my career, I miss you. Additionally, I would like to thank the following individuals who helped me through the writing process: Andy Higgins, Tad Siminitz, Palma Bickford, Charles Lin, and Mark Dudding; Bart Lautenbach and Adam Hannah for their support and giving me the time to do the writing; Tim for including me as an author and for his tireless efforts in editing my content; my family including my mother, Donna, I love you Dad, my brother Gary, sisters Debbie, Dara, and Denise; and finally my love to Kylie, Jacob, and Jolie for being so patient with daddy as he was taking time away from "play" to write this book.

Jaya Nampalli is a Managing Consultant for IBM Software Services for Collaboration. She is responsible for the development of high quality solutions for IBM customers in response to specific business requirements. She is a technical lead developer working on solution feasibility studies or requirements analysis, application assessments, custom design, implementation, testing, and system integration. She works with clients to facilitate the execution of information strategies that are innovative and well aligned based on a client's business needs. At IBM, she considers working on the IBM Centennial project as one of the highlights of her career. Jaya has worked on both small- and large-scale projects. Jaya stays current with web technology advances and other IBM product offerings by self-education and collaborating with other IBM team members. Jaya has been an IBM employee for over 12 and half years.

I wish to thank, first and foremost, Tim Speed for giving me this opportunity to help him write this book. This would not have happened without his support. A very special thanks to my mentor, Raj Balasubramanian, for guiding me to grow both personally and professionally. Also, for motivating me to think beyond my potential.

Also, thanks to the IBM management team that provided approval to publish this book: Walter L Berthelsen, Jack Shoemaker, Luis Pineda, Mark Guerinot, and thanks to our sponsor, Steve Robinson. Thanks to Steve Robinson for writing the foreword on this book. Thanks to the Packt team for their help and support, specially Anugya Khurana and Martin Bell.

A very special thanks to my family for always being there for me. Also, I send thanks to Linda Speed for helping me with this book and providing some of the editing throughout the chapters. I would like to express my gratitude to Jon Czernel for encouraging me to do things beyond my regular scope of work.

Other acknowledgments include: Pam Fryer, Melanie Skinner, Louis Stanley, Leslie Hans, Brad Schauf, David Byrd, Robert Thietje, Stephen Cooke, Marc Galeazza, John Murphy, Barry Rosen, David R. Hinkle, Doug Parham, Gary Ernst, Kevin Mills, and Hunter Medney.

About the Reviewers

Michael Clarkson is an experienced IT and Security Architect with more than 20 years IT experience for large blue chip organizations, and over 13 years experience in enterprise mobility, security, and infrastructure solutions, he has experience in all aspects of mobile technology.

He has previously held roles as a Principal Architect at Sun Microsystems and Oracle, and now works as an independent consultant in mobile solution architecture and technology consulting, providing expertise in the subject of mobile technologies (mobile consumerization, mobile device management, mobile OS vulnerabilities, and so on).

He currently holds the following industry certifications: Certified Information Systems Security Professional (CISSP), TOGAFv9 Practitioner, ISEB Enterprise & Solution Architecture Practitioner, Informa Telecoms & Media Academy – Diploma in Mobile Communications (Distinction), ITILv3, Prince2, Sun Solaris SCSA.

Jason Slater is a technology journalist, blogger, and software developer with over 25 years industrial experience building, managing, and writing about scalable distributed and web-based applications. Jason is a member of the British Computer Society and holds a Master's degree in Computer Science (Internet technologies) with Distinction.

Jason is the editor of a popular technology blog (http://www.jasonslater.co.uk) and is a regular contributor to technology publications, radio, and television. Jason founded Micromicon Media Limited (http://www.micromicon.com) in 2010, which builds mobile apps and helps people with their Web and technology problems.

You can reach and follow Jason on Twitter @jasonslater.

www.PacktPub.com

Support files, eBooks, discount offers and more

You might want to visit www.PacktPub.com for support files and downloads related to your book.

Did you know that Packt offers eBook versions of every book published, with PDF and ePub files available? You can upgrade to the eBook version at www.PacktPub.com and as a print book customer, you are entitled to a discount on the eBook copy. Get in touch with us at service@packtpub.com for more details.

At www.PacktPub.com, you can also read a collection of free technical articles, sign up for a range of free newsletters and receive exclusive discounts and offers on Packt books and eBooks.

http://PacktLib.PacktPub.com

Do you need instant solutions to your IT questions? PacktLib is Packt's online digital book library. Here, you can access, read and search across Packt's entire library of books.

Why Subscribe?

- Fully searchable across every book published by Packt
- Copy and paste, print and bookmark content
- On demand and accessible via web browser

Free Access for Packt account holders

If you have an account with Packt at www.PacktPub.com, you can use this to access PacktLib today and view nine entirely free books. Simply use your login credentials for immediate access.

To Linda, my favorite wife

— Tim Speed

To Bonnie and Josh, my life began on the days you were born

— Darla Nykamp

To my family

— Jaya Nampalli

Table of Contents

Preface

Welcome to the world of mobile devices. Very soon there will be more smart devices than there are people on the planet Earth. Today, nearly every individual uses some kind of mobile device. This is a wonderful time and devices are today's future now. This book, *Mobile Security: How to Secure, Privatize, and Recover Your Devices*, will not only introduce you to this wonderful mobile world, but also help you manage the basic risk that comes with these devices. This book also covers the topic of the day, privacy. This book will provide you with a step-by-step template on what you need to do to protect yourself, and will also give you instructions on what to do if you have an issue with your device.

What this book covers

Chapter 1, Living in a Mobile World, starts by taking you down the road of mobile devices. We cover how mobile devices are used, definitions like BYOD, and a bit of history. All of this information is to get you ready to understand how to best use your device.

Chapter 2, Users and Mobile Device Management, talks about MDM, which may be a new concept to many device users. MDM is used by many companies in order to keep a firewall between the device and the corporate network. MDM is also used to manage devices and make sure that your device does not adversely impact the corporate network.

Chapter 3, Privacy – Small Word, Big Consequences, talks about privacy, which is a very important consideration in the world of "instant" data. You can Google yourself and find all types of information about you. This chapter will help you understand your Internet identity as well as understanding the type of data that can be found about you.

Chapter 4, Mobile and Social – the Threats You Should Know About, will help you to understand the various scams and social engineering that can impact you. We all live in a social world of Facebook, LinkedIn, or even IBM Connections. These very cool tools can also be used against you. Let's not forget the cloud, another great feature of the social world, but it also has its risks. We will show you how to safely navigate this social world.

Chapter 5, Protecting Your Mobile Devices, shows you the various features smart devices provide that can help you keep your device safe. This can include how to create "good" passwords, using encryption, and whom to contact if you have a problem.

Chapter 6, Support and Warranty Insurance, talks about insurance and support, which can be very confusing. You may get your device from one vendor, your phone service from another, and your e-mail from another. This chapter will show you what you need to do if you have an issue. Also discussed in this chapter is the extended warranty.

Chapter 7, Baby Boomers, Teens, and Tweens – Sorry, we don't have next week's lottery numbers, but we can tell you that the growth of smart mobile devices is significant. Mobile-based solutions using small handheld devices are becoming the standard for personal and business use. In the future, more and more computing will be conducted via these small devices. This chapter will show you what is upcoming and its impact.

Chapter 8, Getting Your Life Back After You've Been Hacked, is not only a summary of what has been reviewed in this book, but most importantly this is a checklist of steps that the end user can use in order to get their life back if they are hacked or if their device is lost.

Appendix A, IBM Notes Traveler, explains the IBM Notes Traveler software, which is a mobile device product that provides access to IBM Lotus e-mails. This product, along with IBM Domino, provides an end-to-end solution for mobile access to corporate e-mail via a mobile solution.

Appendix B, Mobile Device Management, is an advanced chapter that shows the management side of MDM, while *Chapter 2, Users and Mobile Device Management*, shows the end user impact. This appendix shows the solutions and choices for a corporate environment.

Appendix C, Tips to Help You Protect Your Mobile Device, is a supporting appendix for *Chapter 3, Privacy – Small Word, Big Consequences*.

Appendix D, Mobile Acceptable Use Policy Template, discusses the Mobile Acceptable Use Policy (MAUP) document that many companies ask end users to sign. This "sample" template is provided as part of this book in order to show you, the end user, what you may need to sign. Also, the MAUP template may be used by a company as a starting point to create a corporate Mobile Acceptable Use Policy for enterprise rollout.

Appendix E, The History of Social Networking, the Internet, and Smartphones, provides additional information about the history of the Internet and mobile technologies.

What you need for this book

In order to use this book you need:

- A desire to learn about how to keep yourself safe using your mobile device.
- A mobile device.
- Time – take time to follow the steps and ask for information. *Chapter 8, Getting Your Life Back After You've Been Hacked*, is not only a great summary chapter, but also provides a table that you should fill out (keep it safe and don't post it on a social site).

Who this book is for

This book is primarily for you, the person that has a smart device. The appendices have a few sections that include more advanced information on Traveler and MDM. But overall, this book is for anyone that would like to stay safe using their mobile device.

This book provides details on the threats that are manifested daily in our Internet world. Also, this book provides a special list of actions you can take to protect yourself.

Conventions

In this book, you will find a number of styles of text that distinguish between different kinds of information. Here are some examples of these styles, and an explanation of their meaning.

Code words in text are shown as follows: "In this case, we've used `example.com` to test the QR codes."

New terms and **important words** are shown in bold. Words that you see on the screen, in menus or dialog boxes for example, appear in the text like this: "Enter the information you wish to encode into the QR box, and click on the **Submit** or **Generate** button."

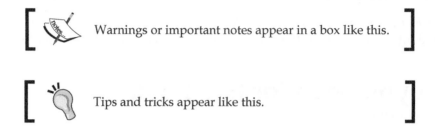

Warnings or important notes appear in a box like this.

Tips and tricks appear like this.

Reader feedback

Feedback from our readers is always welcome. Let us know what you think about this book—what you liked or may have disliked. Reader feedback is important for us to develop titles that you really get the most out of.

To send us general feedback, simply send an e-mail to feedback@packtpub.com, and mention the book title via the subject of your message.

If there is a topic that you have expertise in and you are interested in either writing or contributing to a book, see our author guide on www.packtpub.com/authors.

Customer support

Now that you are the proud owner of a Packt book, we have a number of things to help you to get the most from your purchase.

Errata

Although we have taken every care to ensure the accuracy of our content, mistakes do happen. If you find a mistake in one of our books—maybe a mistake in the text or the code—we would be grateful if you would report this to us. By doing so, you can save other readers from frustration and help us improve subsequent versions of this book. If you find any errata, please report them by visiting http://www.packtpub.com/submit-errata, selecting your book, clicking on the **errata submission form** link, and entering the details of your errata. Once your errata are verified, your submission will be accepted and the errata will be uploaded on our website, or added to any list of existing errata, under the Errata section of that title. Any existing errata can be viewed by selecting your title from http://www.packtpub.com/support.

Piracy

Piracy of copyright material on the Internet is an ongoing problem across all media. At Packt, we take the protection of our copyright and licenses very seriously. If you come across any illegal copies of our works, in any form, on the Internet, please provide us with the location address or website name immediately so that we can pursue a remedy.

Please contact us at `copyright@packtpub.com` with a link to the suspected pirated material.

We appreciate your help in protecting our authors, and our ability to bring you valuable content.

Questions

You can contact us at `questions@packtpub.com` if you are having a problem with any aspect of the book, and we will do our best to address it.

1

Living in a Mobile World

Smartphones are the essential devices of the modern mobile world. We use smartphones to tackle seemingly limitless tasks such as texting, chatting, shopping online, updating our social networking status, researching, emailing, creating documents, making phone calls, video conferencing, and banking. The list will only grow as smartphone capabilities continue to expand. 50.4 percent of US consumers own a smartphone; a percentage which is projected to increase as it has, every previous year (`http://techcrunch.com/2012/05/07/nielsen-smartphones-used-by-50-4-of-u-s-consumers-android-48-5-of-them/`).

Smartphones are attractive devices that can simplify many of our most essential and mundane tasks. Not only do they allow us to connect and interact with others in a simplified manner, but they also allow us to conduct many essential business tasks without the need for comparatively bulky laptops. However, in addition to the seeming wealth of capabilities provided by these devices, smartphones also carry a certain number of risks.

The dangers of mobile computers

Most consumers are aware of the risks that viruses and malware pose for computers, but how many are aware that smartphones are vulnerable to the same sort of pernicious attacks? In a study in the year 2012, antivirus program developer McAfee found that 19.32 percent of consumers either had disabled or nonexistent antivirus software. Assuming that this figure is correct, the vast majority of computers in the United States do possess some sort of active antivirus software. Therefore, most consumers in the US are aware of the risks posed by malware and viruses, and take active steps to protect themselves against such risks.

Compare this with the percentage of smartphones that do not possess some form of antivirus protection, that is, 40 percent. Even worse little more than one third of iPhone users actually have antivirus software installed on their device. Why? According to a research firm, Kaspersky, this is because mobile users feel relatively safe. Many consumers underestimate the danger that malware and viruses pose for their smartphones, even while they recognize the similar risk malicious software poses for their personal computers (`http://www.kaspersky.com/au/about/news/press/2012/number-of-the-week-40-percent-of-modern-smartphones-owners-do-not-use-antivirus-software`).

A widespread lack of awareness

When we consider the number of reported malware attacks, the lack of awareness on the part of consumers becomes truly alarming. Between January and June 2012, Kaspersky recorded over 50,000 malware or virus attacks on smartphones. The number of attacks between January and March eclipsed the number of attacks for the entire year of 2011. In other words, there is a staggering amount of malware programs targeted at smartphones and that number is multiplying at an alarming rate (`http://www.kaspersky.com/images/Kaspersky_Lab_Infographics_Android_Malware_Growth_2012-10-156085.png`).

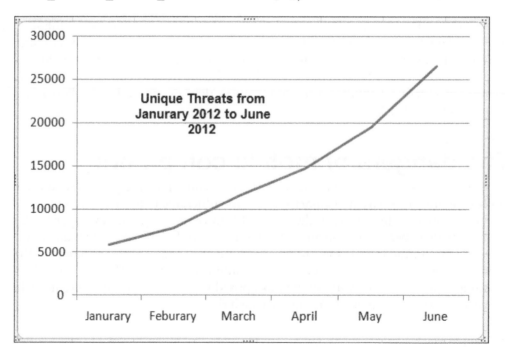

Malware and viruses

Because of the nature of smartphones as multi-purpose devices, the risk posed by malware or viruses can manifest in surprising ways. Consider the Geinimi Trojan, a malware that is embedded in certain apps and games. For a user to contract this Trojan, all they need to do is download an infected application. After installing the app, the Trojan allows hackers to remotely control the device; these criminals can use smartphones to place phone calls, send and delete text messages, and even locate the device geographically using the phone's maps application via the **GPS (Global Positioning System)** functionality that is embedded in the device. If the smartphone's owner had been using the device to conduct mobile banking, then the hackers would even be able to access their banking account or to record their account information. Once the customer data has been identified or captured, then the hacker can send the data back to the "mother ship" via a number of mechanisms, including e-mail and/or text messages (http://www.nbcnews.com/technology/technolog/smart-phone-malware-six-worst-offenders-125248).

Understanding legitimate programs

Malware and viruses represent a significant risk for smartphones; a risk of which many consumers remain unaware. Unfortunately, this threat to smartphone security is not limited to illicit programs, such as malware or viruses. Legitimate programs produced by respected companies are also used to collect and disseminate our personal information. In addition to the well-known companies such as Facebook, smartphone-specific companies, such as our cell phone carriers, also track and monitor our usage. Occasionally, these companies even sell this information, thus further removing our ability to control our privacy. All of this means that containing security risks to our smartphone is not as simple as downloading and installing an antivirus program. In fact, many antivirus products for smartphones are relatively ineffective at stopping threats (http://www.msnbc.msn.com/id/45292075/ns/technology_and_science-security/t/study-some-free-android-anti-virus-apps-fail-miserably/#.UPRrEYYkKSo).

While risks to our smartphone security may seem daunting, there are steps that consumers can take to protect their devices. Using this book, we will teach you how to protect yourself against threats to your smartphone, as well as how to respond in the event that you become a victim of an attack.

Precursors to the smartphone revolution – Internet, social-networking, and spam

By and large, the conveniences we enjoy on our smartphones duplicate the tasks we could only do previously on our laptops and desktops. From tweets to spam, it all started on our computers, and only later moved into the mobile space.

Social networking

Facebook was not the first social networking site. Social networking, or the concept of using the Internet to form relationships and keep in touch with friends, may have begun as early as the mid 90s when sites such as `Classmates.com` and `Geocities.com` first gained prominence.

Facebook, the successful social networking site, was launched in 2004. Many of us already know the story of Facebook and its founder. Facebook originally began as a social networking site exclusive to Harvard students and alumni, but later expanded; first to all universities, and then to the general public. Today, Facebook has evolved into a complex and effective site which allows people to connect with one another in the online space. Members are no longer necessarily required to find and create their own friends network; Facebook has algorithms and automated processes which attempt to find friends for its members. In addition to the basic degrees method first pioneered by Friendster, Facebook also attempts to connect people based on criteria such as hobbies and geographical location.

The method by which Facebook collects this sort of information has even begun to expand beyond the details explicitly provided by members in their profiles. For example, Facebook has developed methods for monitoring external sites that its members visit. One that many may be aware of is the Facebook icon that adorns many websites. If a user clicks on one of these buttons, this provides Facebook with a method of linking a member's interests to their profile. What's more, this is done even if a Facebook member did not intend to provide such information to the site.

In 2006, Twitter launched with the concept that social networking may be best enjoyed in a smaller and more digestible format. Twitter's approach to social networking created a multi-layered network, whereby a visitor would easily be able to read both a particular member's post as well as the posts of that member's followed accounts. Of all of the social networking sites, Twitter may have been the most successful in the migration to the mobile space. The reason for this should be understandable; the screens on smartphones are smaller than laptop or desktop screens, and smartphones are often used in far more limited durations than computers.

The two-way street of social networking

It is important to remember that social networking is a two-way street. Users sign up for these services so that they can interact with friends and colleagues. However, many social networking sites are interested in collecting our personal information. As part of the relationship between users and social networking sites, users routinely provide personal information to these sites. Because social networking sites are businesses, they often consider customer information as one of their most valuable commodities.

With customer information, social networking sites are able to target their customer demographics for presentation to potential advertisers. In some cases, these sites even turn customer information into a commodity by selling it to other companies or parties. Finally, this information is useful as a method for pinpointing demographic deficiencies; Facebook, for example, may decide to expand its marketing for 21 to 45 year olds if it discovers a shrinking user base in that demographic.

This is important to you, the end user, because these practices place your personal information at risk; remember that protecting your information is one of the primary objectives in mobile and electronic security. As will be discussed in *Chapter 3, Privacy – Small Word, Big Consequences*, social networking sites do not always use personal information in the way you might intend. Also, these sites routinely share user's personal information with numerous third parties, thus further decreasing a user's ability to control their information.

2012 is the new 1984 – how companies track us

Companies have always been interested in the demographics of their customers. Before the rise of the Internet, one of the more common methods of assessing customer demographics was through polling. A company spokesman might contact a customer after they have purchased a product or service and ask the customer about their experience. The company spokesman would then use this polling information to create a profile which might represent hundreds or even thousands of potential customers; demographic information, such as race, gender, income level, geographic locale, and personal hobbies or interests might all be incorporated into such a profile.

Today, companies still create exactly these sorts of profiles, but their methods for collecting our demographic information might be surprising; they do so by tracking our computer and smartphone activities. Do you shop on Amazon or at the online stores for Target or Walmart? Do you download music through iTunes? How about social networking sites? Do you use Facebook, LinkedIn, or Twitter? If the answer to any of these questions is yes, then you have provided some or all of these companies with demographic and personal information about yourself. Just like the polls mentioned previously, many company websites use monitoring algorithms to collect information on their visitors in an effort to understand their demographics. So, you might be wondering; how do they get this information? You may think that because you didn't purchase anything from Amazon or because you provided incomplete or inaccurate information on your Facebook account, that the company does not have your personal information. However, you would be surprised at exactly how much information a company is able to collect regardless of what you choose to provide. For example, you may have only browsed the products on `Amazon.com`, but not actually purchased anything. What you may not know is that sites, such as Amazon often have monitoring algorithms that trace their visitors back to their geographic point of origin. What's more, by browsing for certain items, Amazon can infer what age group you're likely to be in, what your gender is likely to be, and even whether you're married or have children. This may not worry you, but consider this; if you have an account on Amazon, they can use this information on your browsing habits to target you for particular sales. Some companies, though not necessarily Amazon, even sell these profiles to other companies.

Facebook and customer tracking

The tracking habits of social networking sites can be even more worrisome. Let's consider the activities of Facebook. As a part of a Facebook profile, a user is requested to provide numerous personal details, including age, race, sex, marital status, geographic location, alma mater, and so on. Many users do not complete all of this information, choosing only to provide those details that they consider necessary for connecting with their friends. However, what many of us don't know is that Facebook can infer some of these details because the site monitors both your activities and the activities of your network of friends. The company can infer, for example, your geographic location based on the geographic location of your friends.

The danger of this sort of a practice has, unfortunately, been demonstrated by several scandals that have marred Facebook's reputation in recent years. In 2007, Facebook launched **Facebook Beacon**, which was a system that monitored the activity of Facebook members both within their profiles and through external sites, such as Fandango. What this means is that, if you purchased some tickets through Fandango, Fandango might, as a partner with Facebook Beacon, send this information to Facebook. The purpose of Facebook Beacon was to target advertising efforts to their members. Facebook addressed privacy concerns by arguing that no information was collected without a member's explicit approval, but they failed to specify that such approval was interpreted through acceptance of the privacy agreement. Practically, this means that every Facebook member's personal information could be collected and released to other Facebook partner companies, because everyone with a Facebook account was required to accept the privacy agreement upon signing up (`http://www.zdnet.com/blog/btl/facebook-beacon-update-no-activities-published-without-users-proactively-consenting/7188`).

Though Facebook Beacon was discontinued not long after its launch, other privacy scandals have continued to rock the company. In 2012, a number of users discovered that what they thought were private messages were appearing publicly on timelines (`http://hypervocal.com/news/2012/facebook-bug-hack-private-messages-timeline/#`). In 2011, Facebook even had to settle a lawsuit with the **FTC**, admitting that they had engaged in deceptive privacy practices; between 2007 and 2011, Facebook had altered their privacy agreement numerous times. Some have argued that this practice was an attempt to mislead users about their privacy rights. After all, how many of us really read the privacy agreements on websites, such as Facebook in any great depth before clicking on **Accept**? The manner by which these same companies, as well as hackers and other criminals, track our activities on smartphones and other mobile devices is covered in greater detail in *Chapter 3, Privacy – Small Word, Big Consequences*.

The new mobile world

Throughout the 90s, computer and Internet technology revolutionized the way we socialized, purchased goods, and even found employment. By the end of the decade, many essential tasks could be completed without the need to leave the comfort of our homes. New concepts like "social networking", "telecommuting", and "digital goods" entered our collective vocabularies. Smartphones may represent a natural evolution of this process. While shopping for Christmas gifts from the comfort of our homes can be convenient, it can be even more convenient to shop for Christmas gifts from a smartphone while away from home. However, these new capabilities can be something of a double-edged sword; in some ways, smartphones are more vulnerable than laptops that have traditional antivirus software.

Making a smartphone smart

Originally, smartphones were any cell phones designed to perform tasks in addition to just making phone calls. These early smartphones had a dedicated and limited operating system. Today, however, smartphones are a specific class of device with a broad array of capabilities and features; what this is means is that the operating systems on smartphones are similar to the fully featured operating systems, such as Windows that run on our computers. Regular cell phones, by contrast, run on **Real Time Operating Systems** (**RTOS**) operating systems, which possess more limited capabilities and are designed to be more streamlined in nature. A smartphone is merely a mobile phone/cell phone that has more advanced computing capabilities, connectivity, and functionality than a conventional phone, which is limited in functionality to a basic handset or feature phone. The latter usually having the ability to run the third party apps via J2ME or BREW, but which have limited integration with the phone capabilities. Smartphones, on the other hand, usually have more advanced APIs that allow the third party apps to have tighter integration with the phone features and capabilities. Beyond this basic requirement, the variety of functions that smartphones can perform is seemingly limitless. Smartphones can organize our calendar and fax our documents, but they can also be used to update our Facebook status, download movies, and countless more functions through a variety of applications. You might say that this is what makes them smart; their focus on their additional functions as opposed to their ability to serve as mobile telephones.

The iPhone – why every phone secretly wants to be a smartphone

The iPhone is the elephant in the room when it comes to smartphones. According to a report by technology publication Engadget, the iPhone commanded a staggering 34.3 percent of the cell phone market share in the US as of October 2012 (http://www.engadget.com/2012/10/02/comscore-iphone-moved-up-to-34-percent-us-share-in-august/).

When you consider that the remaining market share is spread out across all other cell phone manufacturers, from Samsung to Motorola, you can see why Apple's competitors might be envious of the iPhone's success. After all, according to Engadget, three out of every ten cell phones in the US are iPhones. But this data is changing quickly. Smart mobile devices, including notebooks, smartphones, and tablets, shipped 308.7 million units during the first quarter of 2013. This shows a net increase of 37.4 percent over the figures compiled from the previous year. The Android operating system, accounted for a hefty 59.5 percent. Apple's iOS took 19.3 percent of the market share, just 1.2 percent ahead of Microsoft's share of 18.1 percent.

Released in 2007, the iPhone was originally conceived as an iPod with the added functionality of a cell phone. The original iPhone could make and receive phone calls, but it could also play music and interact online. Subsequent iterations of the iPhone only cemented the success of the first release. In July 2008, Apple released the iPhone 3G. The primary feature of this device was in the title; it ran on the third generation of the mobile telecommunications network. The iPhone 3G was also the first generation of the device to include GPS functionality and included a maps application.

As you can see, in the years since the iPhone's release, functionality has been expanded that might allow the device to be easily tracked and monitored. Of course, users benefit from this functionality because they are able to find their iPhone, should they misplace it or should it be stolen. However, other parties may be able to use this same functionality. As will be discussed further in *Chapter 3, Privacy – Small Word, Big Consequences*, Apple is able to use the GPS functionality to track your phone's geographical location. Ostensibly, this is only for the purposes of targeted advertising and customizing consumer support. However, even if you consider Apple to be a trustworthy company, their ability to track your phone's location does render you vulnerable to an outside party. In addition to legitimate parties, such as corporations, illegitimate parties may also be able to utilize these new features. Consider that a hacker may be able to locate your phone geographically through the iPhone's **Find my iPhone** cloud feature; all a hacker would need is your user identification information and a working knowledge of iTunes (`http://ign.com/articles/2010.06/24/the-history-of-the-iphone`).

The difference between Android and iOS

Most of Apple's competitors use the Android mobile operating system to run their user interface.

Comparatively, the iPhone runs on **iOS (iPhone Operating System)**. This is Apple's internally developed operating system, which cannot be used to operate other devices without Apple's permission (and Apple has not, as of the time of this writing, provided such permissions to any other manufacturers). From the perspective of maintaining your mobile security, this is significant because Apple is the sole entity which is able to operate and monitor this platform. Apple protects this operating system (OS), so that it is not easy for the standard end user to alter and/or modify the OS. The best way to understand the difference between the Android and the iOS operating systems for smartphones is by considering the difference between the Windows and Apple operating systems that run on PCs and Macintosh computers. The latter, like iOS on iPhones, only runs on Apple products. The former, like the Android, runs on a variety of devices produced by a variety of manufacturers.

The Android operating system, like the iOS on iPhone, is an operating system designed for the use on smartphones with a multi-touch screen. The Android operating system is currently open source, which means that anyone can access the code and make alterations. What this means for the consumer is that the Android operating system can run quite differently on different phones that use it.

The Android OS is being used in a variety of electronics, including laptops, TVs, cameras, smart glasses, treadmills, headphones, and many other items. This is due to the customizable open and native nature of the Android operating system. One cool use of Android is the **Android@Home** technology that provides home automaton. This technology provides a mechanism to remotely manage smart house devices, including:

- Thermostats
- Power sockets
- Light switches
- Scheduling for powered devices
- Using an Android OS these home services allows end users to manage their home devices using a PC, phone, or tablet

As one might imagine, this lack of parity between the Android phones can also create some problems for the end user, in terms of performance and functionality. Some apps purchased on the Android App Store may only work on certain phones, and thus it is the user's responsibility to ensure that their phone can run the application in question before they choose to download it.

Google introduced a security service to automatically scan applications that are posted in the Google Play Store known as bouncer. This service reviews the applications to determine if there are any malicious applications. This service is not a 100 percent solution and there is no guarantee that this will block all malicious applications. The bouncer program does the following:

- As soon as an application is uploaded into the Google Play Store, the bouncer program starts to analyze the application for known spyware, malware, and Trojans
- Based on a set of rules, the bouncer program looks at an application for any code that may cause issues with the OS
- Also the bouncer program will review the uploaded application against other applications to identify possible issues
- There is also an emulation process that Google executes to determine how the application may run on the Android OS
- The bouncer program will also check the hosting account to determine if this account is known for posting a bad code

Because of the open source nature of Android, Android phones are at a greater risk to security infringements than the iOS phones. According to Bloomberg news, Android phones are far more vulnerable to malware and virus attacks than the Apple devices (`http://www.kansascity.com/2011/11/15/3267279/android-more-virus-prone-than.html`). The primary reason for this is the lack of a rigid infrastructure like the one that exists with Apple's products. While you may utilize Google's official Android App Store to purchase apps, you may also choose from half a dozen other application markets that are available for Android users (`http://www.techrepublic.com/blog/smartphones/iphone-or-android-five-questions-to-help-you-decide/4456`). The oversight on these alternative application markets varies, which means a user may be less assured that a particular app does not contain a virus or malware.

Mobile purchasing and identification methods – who needs credit cards?

Social networking and shopping aren't the only things that have gone mobile. Just as other activities have been modified for the mobile space, so have our identification and payment methods. If a customer is not physically present, but is instead ordering an item through a virtual store accessed by their smartphone, how can they present their ID?

CueCats and QR codes

There was a time when, if someone wanted to purchase something, they might write a check. By the late 1990s, checks had been largely replaced by credit cards for most transactions. In either case, however, a customer would often be asked to provide a form of ID such as a driver's license to verify that the name on the check or credit card was their own. The next evolution in this vein might well be the usage of smartphones, thus eliminating the need to carry both a credit card and an ID to make purchases.

In 1999, Digital Convergence Corporation released the CueCat. The CueCat was a small device which was, appropriately enough, shaped like a house cat. The purpose of the device was to redirect a user, through scanning a barcode or through an audio tone broadcast during a television program, to a particular website. The idea was that a user could automatically be routed to a website through another medium, such as print or television without the need to enter in a URL or to search for a company through a search engine. While the device was ultimately unsuccessful, it foretold the later developments in the mobile space.

Today, the concept of a barcode containing a variety of personal or company information has evolved into the Personal QR, or **Quick Response Code (QR Code)**. To many, the **Personal QR Code** will look like little more than a random series of black and white pixels within a small box. However, this box can contain a website address, product specifics, or even personal information. Put another way, a QR box can contain any sort of information. So, you might ask, how does one access this information? You may be surprised; all you need is your smartphone.

To enable your smartphone to read the QR boxes, whether it is an iPhone or a Galaxy S, all you need to do is download a QR reader app. There are a bewildering number of apps which can perform this function; a search on the Apple App Store for QR Reader, for example, will yield 559 results. Once downloaded, a user can use this app wherever they see a QR code box. Recently, big-box stores have been the most aggressive in creating these QR boxes for customer convenience; a March 2012 article by consumer advocate website Adage relates how Macy's, BestBuy, and Post Cereals were just a few of the companies that were expanding the QR box usage in their stores and on their products (`http://adage.com/article/digital/qr-codes-gaining-prominence-macy-s-buy-post/149474/`). In the case of Bestbuy and Macy's, the companies attached the QR boxes next to the product information displays in their stores. If a customer so chose, they could scan this box using a QR app on their smartphone and obtain pricing and product information.

Recently, some governments and companies have even begun to use the QR codes for official uses. In China, the tickets for bullet trains have been augmented with a QR code to combat ticket fraud and passenger impersonation. Placed on the bottom-right corner of a ticket, the QR code can contain the passenger's name and more worryingly, the passenger's passport or other personal identification number (`http://www.techinasia.com/qr-train-tickets/`). In 2011, the Royal Dutch Mint even issued an official coin with a QR code which would route a user to a website about the Royal Mint's centennial. The company Hackerspace created the world's largest QR code in 2010 by painting on the top of their company building in Charlotte, North Carolina (`http://www.wcnc.com/news/neighborhood-news/Rooftop-QR-code-in-NoDa-verified-as-worlds-largest-146726605.html`).

Keep an eye out for updates; see `http://www.guinnessworldrecords.com/` for the latest record for the largest QR code.

Creating a QR code is actually a relatively simple process. With the following steps, you can create your own QR code box for personal use:

- First, find a QR code generator online. This can be done by simply searching for one, through the search engine of your choice. `Kaywa.com`, for example, hosts a reliable QR code generator on their website. (`http://qrcode.kaywa.com/`)

- Next, choose what sort of information you wish to enter into your QR code. Different generators will provide you with different categories. Using Kaywa's generator as an example, allows you to categorize your information as a phone number, an SMS text message, a URL, or as a plain text. Enter the information you wish to encode into the QR box, and click on the **Submit** or **Generate** button.

- The QR code should appear on your screen. Where it appears may vary depending on the automated generator you chose.

- Now, you can simply save the image to your hard drive. (Right-click on the image and click on **save as**.)

  The following screenshot shows the basic process:

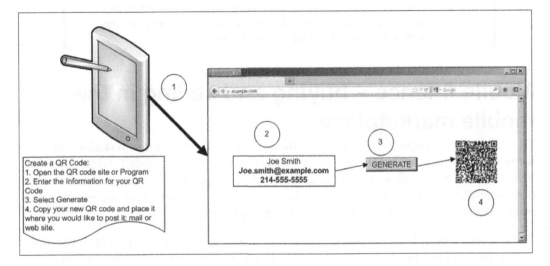

- Congratulations! You have created a QR code. It should look something like this:

Now that the QR box image is saved to your hard drive, all you have to do is choose where to post it. The options are numerous, and should depend upon what sort of information you've chosen to place into your QR code. If the information is about your company or business venture, you might place the QR code on your company's website. If it's a URL for your personal portfolio, you might place the QR code on your resume to allow potential employers a convenient and automated link to your work. The QR box can, as mentioned previously, contain almost any information imaginable. How you use it, of course, is up to you.

 You may notice that we are using `http://www.example.com` as the destination for our QR code. This URL, originally reserved by **Internet Engineering Task Force** in 1999, is a common tool for technology experts when they wish to test certain technologies. In this case, we've used `example.com` to test the QR codes. Did it work for you?

Mobile finance – buying and selling in the mobile marketplace

The advent of smartphones, along with their associated App Stores, has allowed for new methods of monitoring and spending money. While mobile banking has been around for a while now, banks including Chase and Washington Mutual have recently released apps that allow their customers to conduct all necessary transactions from the convenience of their smartphones.

The convenience of this new ability is evident; imagine that you just went to the store to purchase some Christmas gifts, but you didn't remember which account you'd organized the necessary funds for in anticipation of your purchase. Normally, you might have to find the nearest bank branch to check on your balance and rearrange funds. With these banking apps, you can simply log into your account and make the necessary changes while you wait in line to purchase your gifts. Recently, Chase has even added a new feature that allows their customers to transfer funds to other Chase bank customers by simply having their smartphone and the smartphone of their recipient in close proximity. In later chapters, we'll discuss how this convenience carries with it a number of associated risks, and why it may, in some cases, not always be the best idea.

On some occasions, smartphones have even made it possible to purchase goods without needing a credit card or cash. Recently, Salt Lake City has implemented a method of paying for parking by using smartphones. To be able to pay for parking with this method, visitors only need to download the Quick Pay app from the Android or Apple App Stores. After setting up an account through the app, customers can then automate the process through their smartphone (`http://www.deseretnews.com/article/865562673/No-quarters-No-credit-card-No-problem-Just-use-your-phone.html?pg=all`). One early example of using a device for e-commerce is from an example in Asia. In Singapore, one can even buy a Coca-Cola with only your smartphone. This development may be one of the oldest applications of smartphone purchasing possibilities, as it was first introduced back in 2001 (`http://articles.cnn.com/2001-06-20/tech/phone.buys.coke.idg_1_singtel-vending-machines-cell-phone-users?_s=PM:TECH`). Although these purchasing methods have not yet spread to other cities, these practices should still be seen as a sign of things to come; the ease of using a smartphone for transactions may be too alluring for businesses to long ignore.

Because of the bewildering possibilities afforded by App Stores, smartphones are increasingly being utilized as a method of simplifying our most common financial transactions. Today, we can use our smartphones to check our account balance, transfer funds from one account to another, pay for parking, purchase products through various online outlets, and even take payment for goods on those occasions when we are the ones selling goods. Although there are still some limits to what our smartphones can do, we should expect that these limits will only continue to recede as the capabilities of these devices are further realized.

The cloud

Our increasingly mobile world has necessitated new methods of saving and accessing data. Smartphones can be very convenient, as they are mobile and can perform a wide variety of tasks. Unfortunately, smartphones are like computers, vulnerable to data loss through corruption or user error. Additionally, should you forget your smartphone at home, you will be unable to access whatever data it contains until you retrieve it. Cloud technology is an effort to subvert and address these problems.

While the origin of cloud computing is the subject of some debate, the technology was propagated most successfully by Amazon. In 2006, Amazon released **Amazon Web Service**, which is a cloud computing application designed for data retrieval. In the years since, cloud computing has become one of the major sources of innovation in popular computing, being released on consumer platforms, such as iPhone and even game consoles, such as the PlayStation 3.

The essential concept of cloud computing is not, in itself, necessarily a revolutionary idea; data is saved at an external location so that it can be retrieved from numerous devices. What is novel about the concept is that, in addition to data, basic computing and software can also be outsourced and accessed remotely. This means that a user might be able to use a bargain-basement laptop to conduct operations that would require far more powerful and expensive hardware. By outsourcing computing power to an external and more powerful server, such a user would be able to perform power-hungry tasks by connecting to this server over the Internet. This is only one possibility that cloud computing presents; new applications for this model are being developed even as of this writing.

Right now, cloud computing provides some of the following benefits. With cloud computing, if your computer were to crash or if your home burned down, you wouldn't have to worry about losing your data. That, at least, would be recoverable for a reasonable charge. You would only need to access the server from another device, such as a smartphone or laptop, and re-download your data. With the cloud, data is no longer divided by the hard drives of our various devices. Instead, our data can be considered more holistically, and shared among devices as needed to perform various tasks. Put another way, with the cloud, we no longer need to consider one laptop for work and another for home.

For an illustration of how this works in practice, see the following screenshot:

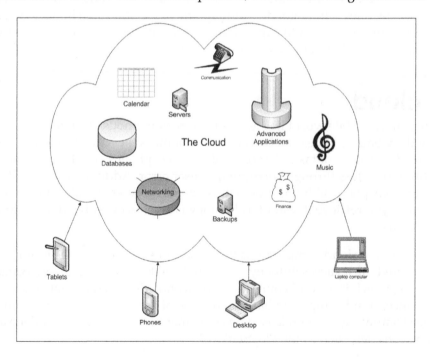

The risks of cloud computing

Although the benefits of cloud computing are numerous, there are also some risks of which we should be aware. Clouds are hosted by an external provider. It is the provider's server, after all, that we use to store our data. Thus, just as we can access our data, so can the provider; how safe the data is depends upon the provider you have chosen. There are safe providers out there, but how do you decide which one to use? It is important that each user conducts some requisite research regarding the security protocols of each provider. Apple's security protocol, for example, which may be found in its service agreement, pays particular attention to those sections which concern the iCloud and user privacy.

Regardless of the service provider, it is important to remember that uploading data to a cloud carries some inherent risks. By deciding to place your data on a cloud, you are sacrificing your ability to control that data. Consider the case of Mat Honan; hackers were able to use some of Honan's personal information to convince both Apple's and Amazon's tech support departments to provide them with Honan's cloud login information. Once they had Honan's login for these services, the hackers were able to access all of the data Honan had chosen to upload to both clouds. Unfortunately for Honan, he had chosen to upload certain sensitive documents that allowed the hackers to extrapolate his login information for his Facebook and Twitter accounts. The result was that Honan's online persona was hijacked because hackers were able to access his cloud data (`http://www.wired.com/gadgetlab/2012/08/apple-amazon-mat-honan-hacking/`). To mitigate the risk of something similar happening to you, it is important to carefully choose which sorts of data you wish to upload to the cloud. Documents or data which contain sensitive personal information should not be considered for upload; should you wish to back up these sorts of documents, you should instead use an external hard drive or thumb drive.

Summary

Our world is increasingly going mobile. Where we once had to use our computer to surf the Internet or had to go to the store to shop, we can now use our smartphone for both. What's more; we can often do these tasks simultaneously. This multi-tasking capability presents the possibility for new takes on old activities. Today, we might go to the store instead of shopping from our computer, but by bringing our smartphone, we're able to compare prices online while we visit the store, so we can touch and see the item we wish to purchase. In other words, we no longer have to choose between visiting the store and shopping online. Smartphones have allowed us to do both simultaneously.

Despite the advantages that this new mobile world offers, it is important to remember that there are also some distinct disadvantages. Facebook, Twitter, Target, Amazon, some government organizations, and even our phone carriers are able to track our activities on our smartphones. This may seem rather innocuous at first glance, but there is more to worry about than simply targeted sales. These tracking methods can be used to spread your personal information to numerous other entities for both legal and illegal purposes. After all, once the information is compiled, it becomes just like any other container of sensitive information; it can be stolen or utilized for purposes that we did not originally intend. Consider your wallet as an example, you keep your driver's license and credit cards in this container so that you can easily access them to purchase items or to prove your identity. However, just like with online data tracking, this wallet can be stolen and used to impersonate you or even be used to steal your resources. In *Chapter 2, Users and Mobile Device Management,* you will learn about the impacts you can experience based on how you company can control your device.

In this chapter, we discussed the ways in which mobile and smartphone technology has changed the way we live. Topics we discussed include:

- Social networking sites
- How sites we visit track us
- The iPhone as the most ubiquitous smartphone
- iOS and Android mobile operating systems
- How commerce is increasingly going mobile, from banking to shopping
- QR codes as a convenient method of creating an identity verifier in the mobile space
- Cloud computing and its applications

Also the specifics of the risks inherent in the new mobile world will be discussed and expanded upon in the later chapters. We are here to help you navigate this social world and to help keep you safe.

2
Users and Mobile Device Management

The world of computing is changing, again. This history of computing is more than just personal computers. It was not too many years ago that punch cards were being used and there were jobs just for people to enter data. Today, we are living in a truly mobile world, complete with a variety of devices that we use for talking, playing games, sending messages, and even work. The important term for this chapter is **Bring Your Own Device (BYOD)** to work. This chapter will focus on the impact of BYOD on the workplace. BYOD brings several impacts to you, as follows:

- Many companies are installing what is known as **Mobile Device Management (MDM)** solutions. This solution is a part of a holistic corporate security policy.

- MDM solutions provide two basic types of corporate security policy management for mobile devices:
    - How to securely access your corporate e-mail: This normally includes specialized network devices and a controlled corporate network
    - A description on what you can do with your device on the corporate network; this is also known as a Mobile Acceptable Use policy

- This discussion on MDM will provide you with information about what you can expect and what a company can do to your tablet and/or smartphone.

Protecting the corporations

Before we go too far, we need to define a few elements for you:

- Corporate security policies
- Corporate security procedures
- Frontend network protection

Corporate security policies

Corporate security policies provide a best practice outline that can be implemented by a company to all their employees. These corporate policies help companies minimize risks and provide a framework on how to respond to security issues or incidents. Corporate security polices can include:

- Rules on how employees connect to the corporate network
- High-level network configuration information
- Security definitions and descriptions on how security issues are managed

Corporate security procedures

Corporate security procedures provide details on how a security policy is implemented. One example is if a mobile device is lost then the company will execute a remote wipe on the device. A remote wipe can remove all the data on the device.

Frontend network protection

Frontend network devices are corporate network components that will help protect the company network from hackers. These frontend devices can help manage inbound Internet traffic and can also help manage smart device access.

Mobile and business

Using a mobile device is not new for business access and/or work. BlackBerry (www. rim.com) devices have been around and have provided e-mail (and application) access for years. The history with most companies is that a BlackBerry device would be provided to the employee, and then the employee would have access to the corporate e-mail and/or application systems. This history also shows that more than one BlackBerry would be presented to a select part of a corporate population. Today's companies have to deal with the fact that mobile devices are being used by more than just salespeople, doctors, and corporate executives.

Now, let's introduce you to your company IT administrator, his name is Roger. Our story is now about you and your new IT friend, Roger. In the following section, we will share this story with you that is very common in many of today's companies.

Buying your device

Off to the mobile store you go; you are buying a mobile device today. You saw the advertisement on the TV and now you must have the new mobile phone/tablet. Now that you have the new device, you are ready to start reading your corporate e-mail and/or accessing the expense system. Being a five year employee at **ACME Anvil Corporation**, you know the head of the corporate e-mail system. You bring your new super tablet to your computer friend and tell him, "put our e-mail on my tablet, please!" As noted, Roger has been your working friend for many years and he is happy to help you. Roger tells you the following rules:

- You need to use a special Internet address: www.mobile.example.com/mailsystem

- Once you connect to your company server, you may need to use your normal username and password (or a special one that was provided by Roger) that you use to connect your PC to the network when you come to work.

- Roger may also say, "Use your one time use **Personal Identification Number** (**PIN**) that I will give you in order to get to the corporate cloud".

- If you lose your device; "Tell me as soon as possible. I will need to wipe it. (remove all the e-mails or all the device contents)", Roger tells you.

- You will be forced to put a device password on your device/tablet.

At this point you stop and ask Roger, "What device password?"

Roger answers your question, by saying, "Now, this gets interesting. Have you ever heard of Mobile Device Management?"

Mobile Device Management

Bringing your own device to work is not totally new. Many employees have been using their own devices, which they themselves purchased, for years. Many companies run software to check a user's computer before the user is permitted to connect to a corporate network. The growth of the home office changed the rules of corporate computing. IBM's policies provide a good example of how home offices can be integrated into the modern workplace; many of the authors of this book have not had a dedicated office space for years. Some companies will allow users to connect with an employee-owned computer from their home, while others will allow only a corporate computer to connect to a corporate network.

One very important point to understand is that the use of BYOD can be different from company to company and also can be impacted via various government rules.

Does your company trust your device?

There is an initial issue with bringing your own device to work (in this case, the corporate network). If the process for BYOD is not managed properly then corporate data could be exposed outside of the trusted network. The authors have worked with many companies where the smart device, with corporate data, is lost. In this case, confidential data that could be stored on the phone is now available to hackers or competitors.

Another big issue is scalability. For example, if one person at a company requests access to the corporate network using a smartphone, then that is normally not a big issue (there is always a security concern). But if there are 10,000 requests, then this becomes a management scaling (running large number of devices) issue. Now, there are issues with the ability to support the users, keep the data secure, and keep a certain access quality service-level.

Most companies provide a basic trust in the employees within a computing environment. Also, these same companies will verify that the computing environment is protected and that the bad people, also known as hackers, don't get into the trusted network.

Internet facing companies have built a strong set of defenses to protect the trusted internal network. These defenses, up to this point, have focused on **Personal Computers (PC)** and not as much on the new smartphones and/or tablets.

Many companies will verify the use of your PC and/or BYOD and then make sure the devices are safe to be used on the corporate environment. This verification process includes: policies, procedures, and specialized products.

As a part of the specialized products that the companies use to protect their frontend network, a device known as Mobile Device Management (MDM) is being installed. The use of a MDM is basically between you and your company, but many companies will not allow access into their network and/or e-mail unless an MDM style product is used. Also, the MDM software is used to verify the use of the mobile device and to help remotely fix any issues that may occur on the device.

Details of MDM

MDM is a product that is normally installed by a specific corporate computing enterprise. Overall end users will not purchase the MDM solutions, but end users will be impacted (and potentially benefited) by MDM.

So, let's jump into MDM; this book is about the end user experience, but we will also share the names of the products. Most end users will not be buying these products but, as noted before, will experience the result of having these products installed. The diagram and description shows how easy it is for you, the end user, to get connected to your corporate computing network.

The following diagram shows the basics of a simple MDM end user access:

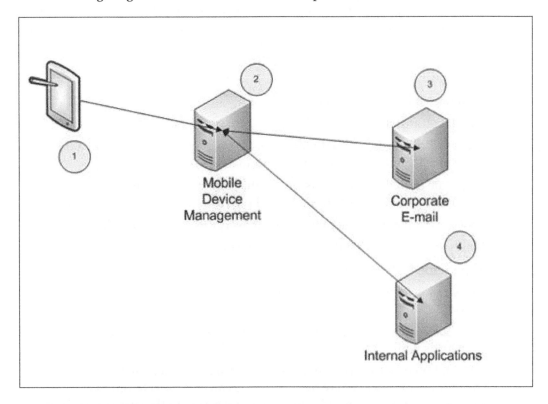

The steps shown in the preceding figure are simple:

1. Open your device.
2. Access the URL from your company.
3. Now it is automatic; the MDM server will access the e-mail.

    Or

    The MDM will access your applications via a set of corporate rules.

Access to your corporate data is very transparent to the end user. Overall you, the end user, will not even notice that your device is being managed by the MDM software.

MDM end user benefits and impacts

Today's MDM solutions will provide organizations with end-to-end security. This is a complex expression, but overall this means that your data is safe (possibly encrypted) from the point it is sent on your device to the mail server way back at the corporate server or the cloud solution that you are using.

MDM features include:

- If a device has been jailbroken or rooted
- Safe data transfer
- Password management: Both for access to your corporate data and a device password; including password lockout management
- Corporate authentication: This can be the same password that you use for your Windows account and/or special passwords
- Configuration management to corporate services, e-mail, and VPN
- Ability to wipe a device if the device is lost or stolen
- Application inventory management
- Policy management: This controls what you can access on the corporate network
- Some MDM solutions provide mechanisms for end users to reset their passwords without having to call a help desk
- A formal process to enrol the devices into the mobile management solution: The enrolment process may require you (as an end user) to put in a temporary password, in order to gain initial access to the corporate server and/or corporate cloud
- Backup and restore: This is a cool feature that many MDMs and cloud solutions include

In some cases companies, via the MDM solution, will automatically install encryption technologies. This technology can provide an end-to-end encryption solution for any data that is sent from your phone to a corporate network. This is not the case with all companies, check with your company and ask if this solution has been enabled for you.

Jailbreak and rooting

When you purchase a mobile device (phone or tablet) you will find that a specific type of software is installed, also known as an operating system (OS), for example:

- Windows Mobile
- IOS (Apple)
- Android

Many of these operating systems are known as closed systems; overall that means that you cannot make changes to the basic software that runs the device. You can still download your applications, games, and e-mail, but you cannot modify the OS and add your custom changes. This OS restriction is there to provide a consistent and secure user experience as well as to protect the end user and to help keep the applications at a high quality.

There have been several postings on the Internet on how to jailbreak your device. This jailbreak process can allow you to install applications that have not been approved applications for that vendor. As a part of this term you will see rooting; this is the same step, removing the protections so additional applications can be installed.

The authors of this book do NOT recommend that anyone jailbreak/root a device.

Digital Rights Management

Many devices include a special layer of software known as **Digital Rights Management (DRM)**. This is a code that protects the device from bad applications. This is one reason not to jailbreak a device. Be sure and understand your rights and/ or your rights based on the country you live in before you make any core changes to the base device.

Check this link for more information about DRM: `http://en.wikipedia.org/ wiki/Digital_rights_management`.

A company may allow an employee to use their own BYOD or issue a device. If the employee then jailbreaks (or roots) the device, then the employee can put the company at risk. Bad software, hacks, and bots can all be infected into the phone and if the end user breaks the security on a device and ignores the DRM, then the company can be put at great risk.

MDM solutions and products

There are several MDM products on the market, the following is a short list for you and your management team to review, if you don't have an MDM solution already:

- Good technology: `http://www1.good.com/mobility-management-solutions/mobile-device-managemen`

- Sybase

- Airwatch: `http://www.air-watch.com/?gclid=CJfsidy0-rMCFc5cMgod7i8AIQ`

- MobileIron: `http://www.mobileiron.com/`

- SmartMan: `http://www.dialogs.de/en_US/produkte/smartman.html?hl=en_US`

- IBM Endpoint Manager: `http://www.ibm.com/`

Acceptable use policy (AUP)

Back to our story, Roger got you connected to the corporate network via your smart device. You now have an e-mail access to the corporate mobile expense system; all is good in your world. Later that day, you receive a message titled **Corporate Mobile Acceptable Use Policy**.

The corporate mobile acceptable use policy is starting to be used by many companies. This policy describes how you can use the device and/or access to the corporate networks. The standard **acceptable use policy (AUP)** normally includes what you can and can't do on the corporate network. Many people find this to be a basic conflict of rights due to the fact that the device was purchased by the end user. This book does not review these rights and please do not send messages to the authors regarding this issue; this is between you and your company.

Most acceptable policies follow a basic format which includes:

- **Purpose**: This is the definition of the AUP and why it is needed.
- **Applicability**: Who does this apply to; employees, contractors, students, guests, and others.
- **Employee responsibility**: It is the responsibility of the employee that uses a mobile device to follow the AUP and/or other corporate rules regarding the corporate networks and/or resources. Also, most AUPs will have rules requiring the employee to keep the device safe.

- **Device impacts**: What are the rules if the device is lost, stolen, or broken? Also many AUPs will include rules that prevent the end user from jailbreaking and/or installing any specific applications. Also there may be rules about software licenses. One big point that AUPs may include concerns what will occur if the device is infected with malware.

- **Malware**: A definition of viruses, worms, and spyware.

- **Corporate rights**: The AUP may define how the company reserves the right to limit and/or refuse the right of any end user to connect to the corporate network and/or resources.

- **Device list**: This is normally a list of devices that are supported by the company.

- **Non-compliance**: AUP will describe the impact to end users if the rules and/or AUP are not followed. Some rules may include having the device cleared (data is wiped off including e-mail and applications). The device may be locked off the system. The end user may be put on suspension and/or terminated.

  This book provides a sample AUP in the appendix.

Power users

A power user is an interesting term; in general a power user is an expert user. This is the person that you would go to and say, "do you know how to do this?" In many cases a power user actually knows what they are doing, while others may guess and mess up your phone. Power users are the ones that install the cool applications and know how to quickly solve simple problems.

Bring Your Own Device is causing several issues with large companies as follows:

- End users call the help desk and will ask how to do simple things on their phones

- E-mail may need to be fixed and/or reconfigured on a device and/or smartphone

- End users may call the help desk and complain about the speed of the connection

Many corporate help desks will not help users on phone questions, for example:

- "How can I install the Angry Birds game?"

  You may agree this is not normally a critical business request!

- But the corporation help desk may answer questions like:

  "My e-mail was working, but now it is not working?"

The end user is getting frustrated and may say, "The help desk is no help; I need Angry Birds." The concept is really lost on most end users, BYOD really means "Bring YOUR OWN Device". The help desk with many companies will not help you install games or even your favorite Star Trek episode. The help desk will help you with business required applications and/or e-mails only.

So what does the end user do? They will ask, "Do you know how ....." This is the birth of the power user. We saw this with PCs and now with mobile devices.

The risk is, not all power users are the same. Here is our story:

Troy really wanted to get Angry Birds installed. So he went to Bob and said, "The help desk will not help me install any games." Bob tells Troy, "I am an expert, bring your device to me."

Bob gets Troy's iPhone and starts making changes. Bob, not being an expert with the iPhone, resets the device to factory mode, losing all of Troy's applications and e-mail. Now, Troy really needs help to get his e-mail and/or corporate expense system back on his device, and Troy still does not have any games.

The moral of this story is, "not all power users are powerful and/or knowledgeable; be careful!"

In the later chapters, we will tell you how to back up your device and how to protect it.

Power user tools

We introduced you to the concept of power users so that you can understand this next section. Most end users will never use these tools. This is an advanced section of this chapter, please be careful; you may end up with a dead device if you are not careful. There are several tools you can use to customize your mobile devices, including the following list of tools:

iPhone configuration tools

The iPhone configuration utility lets the end user create configuration files that can install specialized setup configurations to install applications and manage the device.

These configuration profiles are saved and transferred in a special format known as XML. **XML (Extensible Markup Language)** is a type of coding used for web access via a browser and other technologies. The use of XML and/or iPhone configurator is normally done by administrators and/or real power users.

Two basic terms will be used as a part of using the iPhone configurator, as follows:

- Payload
- Configuration file

A payload is a collection of a specific set of configurations that can be pushed into your iPhone. One example of this is a **Virtual Private Network (VPN)**, which is used to connect to your corporate network via a special set of software and/or hardware.

The configuration profile normally includes several sets of payloads.

You need to tether (connect) your device to a PC in order to use this configuration.

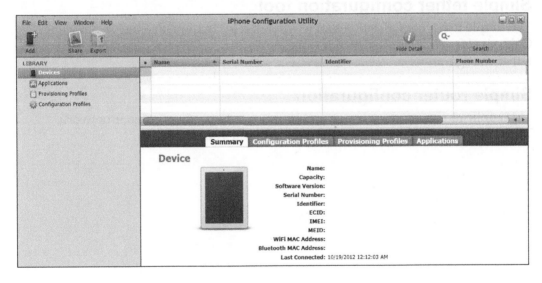

The iPhone configurator is available at `http://help.apple.com/iosdeployment-ipcu/win/1.1/`.

Android configuration tools

The authors found several sets of tools that can potentially be used by power users and/or administrators. These tools are available at `https://play.google.com/store`. Some tools to consider are as follows:

- Configuration
- Simple tether configuration
- Simple router configuration
- Lookout
- Quick settings

Let's review these tools.

Configuration

Configuration is a basic application that will display and save the device configuration. This type of tool can be used by developers to determine what is running on the devices.

Simple tether configuration tool

The simple tether configuration tool was created to circumvent a bug in Samsung Galaxy's software that prevented it from remembering the configuration for a tether configuration.

Simple router configuration

This application is used to change and browse router settings on your network. This application will also scan your system to find your IP routers.

Lookout

Lookout offers essential protection against all the bad stuff that can happen to your phone or tablet, such as malware and viruses, loss, and theft. See the following screenshot for an example:

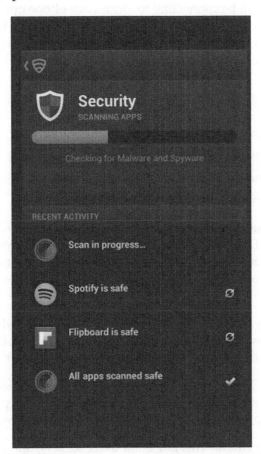

Quick settings

This application provides a quick review of your phone settings.

The hidden world (some advanced information)

Once you connect to your corporate network, you will be connected to a hidden world of network access and protection. Overall, most end users will not care about this world and/or the access connections. This book will show you some of the systems that you will be connecting to, once your phone opens your corporate network. This world is obfuscated from end users and hackers, by design. Each component is installed in order to protect the end user as well as the corporate network and corporate data. Let's review each of the following basic components:

- Firewall
- Reverse Proxy
- Mail Routing Server
- Mobile Device Management
- Application Servers
- Messaging Servers

Firewall: This is the basic frontend interface into the corporate network. Another term you may hear is DMZ. A **DMZ (demilitarized zone)** is a computer network inserted between the untrusted Internet and the corporate, trusted network, as a neutral zone between a company's private network and the Internet. The goal of the DMZ is to prevent unauthorized users from getting access to a corporate service.

Reverse Proxy: This is normally an extension of the Firewall and/or the DMZ. The reverse proxy will provide access to the corporate environment by a pass through a process that will hide the internal servers to the outside Internet world.

Mail Routing Server: This server provides a special access to mobile devices into the corporate mail servers. This is a specialized server that also provides the sync processes used to keep the server in sync with the mobile device.

Mobile Device Management: This is a set of tools, servers, and processes that are used to help manage end user mobile devices. A detailed description on administrative MDM is included in the appendix of this book.

Application Servers: These are the servers that a company will host their corporate applications on, for example, sales tracking and/or accounting tools for mobile devices.

Messaging Server: These are the servers that host a corporation's messaging
e-mail system.

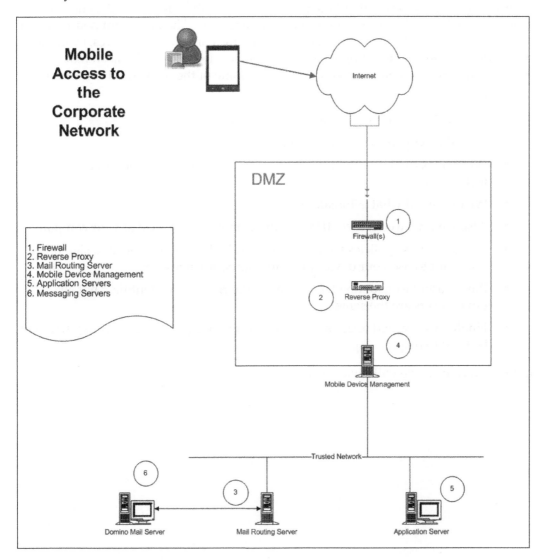

The preceding example shows the sample placements of these components. Keep
in mind that these configurations are not published outside of the corporate
administration teams in each company.

Summary

In this chapter, we learned about the impacts of the mobile device on the end user. This is a very big topic for managers and administrators. The important point for end users is that you can be forced to follow specific rules on your device; yes, even the device that you really own. Bring Your Own Device does not really mean that you can use it for anything on a corporate network. Some of the items we discussed in this chapter included:

- What is MDM and how does it impact you
- Why do companies use MDM solutions
- What rules can be applied (such as passwords) and how you can be locked out
- We discussed what jailbreak means
- Also we reviewed a few MDM solutions that may be used at your company
- Acceptable use policies were reviewed and why you may need to sign one if you want to use your device on your company's network
- Power users were defined and some of the risks were identified; not all power users are the same
- Finally, we learned about some power user tools (or administrators) that may be used to help manage your device

In the next chapter we will review privacy.

3

Privacy – Small Word, Big Consequences

Troy roused from somewhere in the depths of his sleep to silence the alarm on his smartphone. He tried to clear his mind to think. Was this the third or fourth city in 10 days? What city was this, anyway? A quick glance at his calendar app reminded him that he was in Copenhagen, Denmark.

He checked his messages. There were three: his wife had paid his speeding ticket, his flight was on time, and his assistant had scheduled him into a conference call in two hours. It was going to be another busy day.

Troy finished his conference call, called his wife, and headed to the airport. He had already checked in on his smartphone and only had carry-on luggage, so he figured he should be able to speed through the airport. A quick look at his checking account balance assured him his account was fine.

Troy's flight home was a long one, so he connected to the airport's Wi-Fi network and searched for an app to play on the plane. Advanced knitting techniques? No. Multiplication table practice? That would be good for his son. Space motorcycle racing? That would be fun! He downloaded both apps, clicking through the agreement screens quickly.

After landing, Troy rushed through the airport, paid his parking fee with a few quick taps on his smartphone, and headed for the exit. As he drove by a flower shop, he received a spoken text message announcing a 20 percent off sale on roses and a reminder that his mother's birthday was in two days. His mom loved roses, so he made a quick stop at the florist shop and finished his drive home.

Troy and You

Did some of Troy's day sound familiar? Smartphones have become multifunctional tools for many of us. We use them for communicating, surfing the Internet, checking sports scores, and even shopping and banking. Some of these actions can be done semi-anonymously, while others require information about who we are or even sensitive information, such as credit card and bank account numbers. It is the same in the physical world: we can do some activities without anyone knowing who we are, while other activities require us to share very personal information. The digital world generally feels more anonymous than the physical world because it appears we are only interacting with machines. However, the reality is very different.

In the physical world, you are an individual who can be recognized on sight by anyone who knows you. You can prove who you are to those who don't know you by offering proof of identity such as a driver's license or passport. It is your choice when and with whom you share that information. A pickpocket could steal your wallet with your driver's license in it, and your passport. With either item, the pickpocket would know your identity, street address, date of birth, and a few other pieces of information, but that is all. Within minutes, hours, or days, you would know your items had been stolen because you would no longer have them in your possession.

In the digital world, your identity is digital information, which can be copied, combined, analyzed, and tracked. A person anywhere in the world can steal your information by copying it, and then adding it to other information about you. The additional information may have been copied by the same person who previously stole information about you, or it may have been purchased on the Internet black market as part of a set of information on thousands or even millions of people. You may never know your information has been copied unless it is later used to steal your identity. Unlike a missing driver's license or passport, only a copy of the information is taken while the original information remains intact.

With your digital identity, another person, or even many other people, can *become* you. They can obtain credit in your name, buy cars or houses in your name, sell your house (as was done to Roger Mildenhall of South Africa), or even commit crimes while masquerading as you (http://www.identitytheft.info/criminal.aspx). If you have plenty of free time and extra money to spare sorting out messes such as these, then you probably don't need to worry about protecting your digital identity. Otherwise, fasten your seatbelt.

Data good enough to steal

Data on your mobile device is valuable to you for performing your daily tasks and being available for reference when you need it. It is also valuable to others for purposes that may not benefit you.

Cookies, cookies everywhere

When you visit a website, information about your actions while visiting that website is saved. For example, if you visit an electronics store's website and view three flat-screen televisions, the information may be stored regarding the specific televisions you viewed. The information is stored in temporary computer memory called a **session cookie**. The purpose of a session cookie is two-fold: one, to make it easier for you to return to the same televisions if you want to order one, and two, to help the store's website suggest specific items for you to consider purchasing based on what you have already viewed. Once you close the browser, the cookie is deleted.

There are other types of cookies called **persistent cookies**. These are not deleted and can be stored on your computer for months or even years. Generally, these cookies are designed to improve your experience each subsequent time you visit a website. Some cookies, however, are designed for malicious purposes. They may capture information about you with the sole purpose of sending it to a server anywhere in the world without your knowledge or permission. The information captured can include the websites you frequent, your user IDs and associated passwords, and even credit card information you provided to purchase items (http://www.wisegeek.com/what-does-an-adware-tracking-cookie-do.htm, http://www.reputation.com/reputationwatch/articles/how-companies-collect-manage-and-use-your-private-information-when-you-browse-online).

One stolen credit card number can cause you harm, but that can be undone with a call to the credit card issuer. However, a digital file of your actions and multiple credit card numbers built over the course of months or years can be used to develop a profile about you and your very sensitive personal information.

The information captured can be enough for a stranger to duplicate your identity and use your credit or even live as you without your knowledge. The profile built about you can be used to fool people who know you into thinking they are interacting with you via digital means. Some people may even be convinced to drop their guard and provide their own sensitive personal information to your digital twin, who then uses it to start building profiles on your friends. How long will you maintain friendships when the information provided to "you" is used to steal your friends' identities?

They are watching you…and they know your name

The previous paragraph may sound like the start of a movie plot, but it is very real. And it is only one way strangers steal your information. Look at David Crouse's story, documented by The Wall Street Journal. In 2009, David went from a happy man with a solid retirement account and a 780 credit score to a worn out man with drained bank and retirement accounts and a ruined credit score. The entire loss happened in less than six months. What caused this? While visiting a website, malicious software (called **malware**) was secretly downloaded to his computer, which captured every key stroke he made, including credit card numbers and bank account login credentials. His information was then sold to individuals who used it to access his debit card to gamble, make long-distance calls, and buy electronic toys. The charges totaled over $900,000 (http://articles.marketwatch.com/2010-02-10/finance/30765048_1_new-bank-debit-identity).

David Crouse was a victim of identity fraud due to the theft of personal information entered into websites through his personal computer. Identity fraud is defined by the U.S. Department of Justice as "all types of crime in which someone wrongfully obtains and uses another person's personal data in some way that involves fraud or deception, typically for economic gain" (http://www.justice.gov/criminal/fraud/websites/idtheft.html). Javelin Strategy & Research, an oft-referenced research firm, reported that approximately seven percent of all smartphone owners were victims of identity fraud in 2011 (http://spectrum.ieee.org/riskfactor/telecom/wireless/smartphones-becoming-gateways-to-identity-theft). One main difference between David's computer and most smartphones is the level of care people take with the devices and the access to those devices. Personal computers, whether desktop or laptop, tend to be handled carefully when transported and often have antivirus software installed to protect against malware. Smartphones and tablets tend to be tucked into bags or pockets, or left on a nearby table or desk, and frequently contain no antivirus software (40 percent as of May 2012, according to Kaspersky Lab (http://www.kaspersky.com/about/news/press/2012/number-of-the-week-40-percent-of-modern-smartphones-owners-do-not-use-antivirus-software). In addition, according to Javelin Research, 62 percent of mobile device users do not use passwords to protect the contents of their devices. Compared to personal computers, the casual handling and lack of antivirus software make mobile devices more prone to theft, data exposure, and malware.

What's in it for the information thieves?

There is no financial safety net for people like David. He estimated it would take five years to eliminate the debt caused by the identity thieves and save a small amount of his original retirement account. His target age for reaching that goal was 61 years old, leaving him little time to rebuild the funds for the retirement he had planned.

The people stealing and selling David's personal information gained a small amount for their efforts while David suffered a significant loss, which impacted his life for years. Just how much was David's personal information worth? According to MSN Money, the electronic version of a person's credit card information (the type of information captured by malware) is worth between $2 and $90, depending on how many details are available. Physical credit cards using that same information can be purchased for an additional $180. Credentials for logging into a person's bank account can be purchased for $3,500 (http://money.msn.com/identity-theft/what-you-are-worth-on-black-market-credit-cards.aspx). The cost to create and distribute malware is minimal. A thief has only to write the software or obtain prewritten malware from the Internet, and distribute it through e-mails or mobile device software (apps). The thief may even profit from selling the app containing the malware, benefitting twice. One app or e-mail with widespread distribution can install malware on thousands or even hundreds of thousands of devices. And there is an always-ready black market for personal information.

Let's return to Troy's story and the information, which could have been captured during his first waking hours. Malware exists, which will allow a person to take over someone's mobile device, making it possible to record calls and read and send text messages and e-mails (http://spectrum.ieee.org/riskfactor/telecom/wireless/smartphones-becoming-gateways-to-identity-theft).

A stranger using such malware to infect Troy's phone, we'll call him Mr. X, would know that Troy had a significant other, that he had parked illegally in a certain city and incurred a fine for that behavior. Mr. X would also know that Troy had a flight on a particular airline, had a conference call scheduled, that Troy had checked into his flight, and what bank Troy used. Depending on the malware used to steal Troy's data, Mr. X also may have the access credentials to Troy's bank account. What started out as a busy but good day for Troy, has gone decidedly bad.

Good idea, mixed results

Mobile devices are a good idea. They allow us to live untethered to hardwired computers and telephones while remaining in contact with people and information. They allow us to have a pipeline to the world no matter where we are. However, they also allow the world to have a pipeline to us, often without our permission or even knowledge.

Reach out and touch

In a Bell System telephone commercial released in 1979, people were encouraged to "reach out and touch someone". The commercial's intent was to encourage people to spend more time talking to others in distant locations. The creators of that message never intended the action to be harmful, but times have changed and phones, as well as other communications devices, have become a source of potential harm even as they've grown in functionality and use.

Today's devices can function as phones, address books, cameras, Internet browsers, alarm clocks, gaming consoles, personal organizers, libraries, jukeboxes, and financial planners; all while fitting in a pocket or purse. In October 2012, the number of smartphones in use topped one billion globally (http://www.telegraph.co.uk/finance/9616011/Number-of-smartphones-tops-one-billion.html) and 100 million in the U.S. In the U.S., the market was mainly divided between Android (51 percent) and Apple's iPhone (30.7 percent), and smartphones in general contained an average of 41 apps (http://money.cnn.com/2012/05/16/technology/smartphones/index.htm).

With an explosion in the number of smartphones and a dramatic increase in the amount and diversity of data stored in them, the potential for harm has grown in equal proportion. A stranger, copying the information from your smartphone, can know as much about you as you have told the phone. However, unlike the phone, you normally can neither delete your information from the stranger's inventory nor control how it is used.

Touch, but don't break

Apps can be downloaded to devices to perform an almost unlimited number of functions. At the same time, the apps can introduce malware into a device without warning. Because devices are mainly either Apple- or Android-based, the apps are broken into corresponding groups. In the third quarter of 2012, Apple had 250,000 apps available (http://www.apple.com/ipad/from-the-app-store/), while Android apps numbered almost 550,000 (http://www.appbrain.com/stats/number-of-android-apps).

Apple apps may be downloaded only from approved websites unless a device is altered to allow the user to manipulate its operating system. The apps are approved prior to being made available on those websites, although the exact approval process is a tightly-held secret. It was believed for years that this restriction prevented malware from infecting Apple devices. However, early in 2012, unadvertised software was found hidden inside an app without Apple's knowledge and made available from Apple's App Store. The hidden software was not malicious; it simply allowed the user to create an Internet connection. However, it demonstrated to the world that Apple apps were not as safe as once believed, nor inspected as thoroughly as once thought.

Apps may be downloaded to Android devices from approved websites or from independent app providers as long as the device is set to allow the installation of non-Market applications. According to Google's Developer Distribution Agreement, apps offered through Google Play (Google's app market) are not officially approved by Google; Google simply provides the marketplace for the apps. Also, the apps are not necessarily monitored for content, although Google reserves the right to remove an app if it is found to violate laws or Google policies (`http://play.google.com/about/developer-distribution-agreement.html`).

Apps downloaded from independent providers carry an inherent risk of malware. There is also a chance that apps from approved websites contain malware, and that risk is higher than originally thought. During the second half of 2011, the number of unique pieces of malware in Android apps found through sampling increased by 472 percent according to research performed by Jupiter Networks (`http://www.computerworlduk.com/news/security/3319719/google-android-malware-sees-exponential-growth/`).

Apps may appear to be legitimate, yet may actually be counterfeit versions of real apps. Lookout is a leading smartphone security company offering anti-malware and anti-spyware software. Data thieves created an app designed to appear as an update to the Lookout software and embedded malware inside the update app. They posted the app on Google's online marketplace and waited for people to be fooled into downloading it. The malware is able to copy sensitive personal information from Android phones and transmit it to a server in Thornton, Colorado. The information stolen may include messages, video files, and the contents of SD cards (`http://www.pcmag.com/article2/0,2817,2411163,00.asp`).

In addition to potential hidden malware on your device is the possibility of approvals you may have given to an identity thief without being aware you were doing so. These approvals are typically requested as part of the download process. Once you approve, the thief may collect any personal information you enter on your device any time it is entered. Not possible, you say? How closely did you read the permissions you agreed to the last time you downloaded an app? Did any of the permissions seem more extensive than necessary to run the app? Did you download the app from a trusted source? For example, why would a child's puzzle game need access to your address book or calendar?

Looking again at Google's Developer Distribution Agreement, we find a curious section about your personal information. The section begins with standard language warning the developer to protect any personal information collected from users in a manner consistent with most privacy laws. However, later in the section we find this interesting language: "But if the user has opted into a separate agreement with you that allows you or your Product to store or use personal or sensitive information directly related to your Product (not including other products or applications), then the terms of that separate agreement will govern your use of such information." Is it possible you made such an agreement with an app developer while quickly clicking through the agreement screens? If so, you may have given that developer the right to use your personal information, including login credentials and payment information.

And that's only the first part...

Data thieves are not the only ones who can benefit from your information. Legitimate companies also collect and use it for their purposes, and they may not have your best interests in mind.

Hidden "features"

Antivirus and other anti-malware tools will not protect against all malware. The tools can protect you against apps designed to cause harm to your device and steal your data if the apps are recognized as malware by the antivirus vendor. However, there are also valid apps written with "hidden features". These valid apps would not be classified as malware by antivirus software. Some of the hidden features in these apps are harmless, such as the unadvertised app hidden inside the Apple software. Other apps are put there only to benefit the author and those whom the author selects.

Hidden apps may be beneficial to the device's owner, at least when installed. However, over time the functionality of a hidden app may become harmful. For example, the hidden app may contain a vulnerability similar to those found on personal computers, which require software updates to correct. Because the app is hidden, the chance of an update being issued to correct the vulnerability is very small. The vulnerability can be exploited if a hacker learns of it and chooses to use it as a way to gain access to all devices with the app installed.

In November 2011, security researcher Trevor Eckhart exposed a little-known app running on most smartphones (`http://www.networkworld.com/news/2011/113011-mobile-privacy-253621.html`). Eckhart discovered traffic on his company's network that didn't fit expected patterns. By tracing the traffic, he located data being created and routed by an unknown app. The data was coming from colleagues' smartphones and routed to an external company called Carrier IQ (`http://www.foxnews.com/tech/2011/12/06/in-tracking-companies-reveal-their-low-iq/`).

Carrier IQ is the creator of the app and provides it to phone manufacturers, such as AT&T, Sprint, and T-Mobile. The purpose of the app is to help the carriers improve their service to customers by measuring the performance of mobile devices and providing that information to the carriers.

The app has been found on both Android and Apple devices and is configurable to the specifications of individual cell phone providers. Functions of the app include call logging, keystroke monitoring, location monitoring, web browsing history, and application tracking. Before Eckhart's discovery, most smartphone users did not know the hidden app was running on their phones. At that time, the app was installed on over 141 million devices; a number that is growing as more smartphones are sold.

The app is not included in the list of apps active on a phone, so phone users cannot accidently learn about it while viewing phone details. In addition, the app does not include an option to turn it off or remove it from the phone.

The functions of this app already listed allow considerable information to be collected about a person. When the app was discovered, Carrier IQ claimed that none of the information is recorded, stored, or transmitted. One additional function of the app contradicts that claim. The app also allows Carrier IQ administrators to tell the device to contact Carrier IQ, opening a gateway between the phone and the administrator. The administrator can then select data to be sent from the phone to Carrier IQ for analysis. According to a Carrier IQ patent application, the data collected from the phone may include data related "to an end user's interaction with the device... where in the interaction with the device comprises the end user's pressing of keys on the device" (http://www.engadget.com/2011/12/01/carrier-iq-what-it-is-what-it-isnt-and-what-you-need-to/). That sounds very similar to keystroke logging on demand.

Not only is information gathered from phones on demand, the information is sent to Carrier IQ unencrypted, whether or not it is encrypted on the phone. Thus, any protection the phone owner installed to prevent others from viewing information on the phone is lost when Carrier IQ requests transmission of the information.

The fallout

Carriers have stated they use the information collected by Carrier IQ to gather data speed, battery life, and app usage pattern information and to learn what smartphone users do with their phones. Some carriers deny having the app active on their devices, while Carrier IQ lists the carriers as partners.

Concerns over the Carrier IQ app triggered a U.S. Senate investigation and raised questions of potential violations of federal wiretapping laws. In addition, multiple classaction lawsuits were filed against Carrier IQ, Samsung, HTC, Apple, AT&T, Sprint, and T-Mobile (`http://www.forbes.com/sites/ andygreenberg/2011/12/02/and-now-the-lawsuits-class-actions-hit- carrier-iq-htc-and-samsung/`). These actions brought even more attention to the app and prompted frenzied activity to figure out exactly on which devices the app was running.

Gizmodo, a website offering information on technology's current events, created a list by carrier and model of the phones with the app installed. They provided the list to assist the Senate investigation and published it online at this website: `http://gizmodo.com/5868732/the-complete-list-of-all-the-phones-with- carrier-iq-spyware-installed`.

As information on Carrier IQ piled up, it became clear they had been collecting information since 2007; far longer than originally believed (`http://betanews. com/2011/12/16/does-your-phone-have-carrier-iq-now-you-can-know/`).

What does this mean to you? If you own or owned one or more of the smartphones on Gizmodo's list, your personal information, potentially including phone logs, web browsing history, app usage, physical locations visited while carrying your smartphone, and the content of text messages may all be stored in the databases of Carrier IQ and your carrier.

Who has your data? Round 1...

Even the app stores want your data. Who knew a mobile device could make you so popular?

The truth is out there

So far, we have seen that Carrier IQ and your service provider may have copies of your call and text logs and even your text message contents. But it doesn't end there.

The Carrier IQ app is just that, an app. It has the possibility of gathering vast amounts of information about you. Because the Carrier IQ app can do it, so can other apps. Smartphones are equipped with unique device identifiers, which generally cannot be removed. This allows cell phone service providers to recognize your phone. It also allows apps and ad companies to do so.

Studies on Android apps have shown that several apps collect personal information, such as device identifier, passwords, age, gender, contact information, and location. Apps collecting this information often do so without the user's awareness or consent, and frequently transmit the information to other locations, which often mean ad companies. Popular apps found to follow this practice include TextPlus4, Pandora, and Paper Toss. Studies on Apple apps have revealed similar results with even more data being collected and transmitted (`http://timesnewsworld.com/iphone-and-android-apps-collect-and-share-sensitive-user-data-with-advertisers.html`).

MIT researchers studied 36 popular Android apps and found that many of them collected information on users. The guilty app makers included Rovio (developer of *Angry Birds*) and News Corporation (maker of *MySpace*); refer to `http://online.wsj.com/article/SB10001424052748704694004576020083703574602.html`. The apps collected information such as address book contacts, web browsing history, and GPS location whether or not the app was running (`http://malkist.com/mit-finds-android-apps-still-collect-user-data-even-after-shutdown-130184.php3`). MySpace sent age, gender, income, ethnicity, sexual orientation, political views, and parental status.

The **Wall Street Journal (WSJ)** performed an even more in-depth study, evaluating 101 apps for collecting and transmitting device users' personal information. Of the 101 apps, 50 were Android, 50 were Apple, and one was the WSJ's own. Of the 101 apps, 47 transmitted location information and five (5 percent) transmitted age, gender, and other personal information (`http://online.wsj.com/article/SB100 01424052748704694004576020083703574602.html`). If we accept the five percent found in WSJ's study as standard across apps in general, of the approximately 800,000 apps available in the third quarter of 2012, an estimated 40,000 would be transmitting personal information. Some apps transmit location information as often as every 30 seconds (`http://www.bbc.co.uk/news/technology-11443111`).

One Apple app, **Pumpkin Maker**, allows a person to virtually carve pumpkins as part of a game. The app transmits location information without notifying the user or requesting permission. According to the app's developer, he was unaware that Apple required apps to ask a user's approval before taking personal information (`http://online.wsj.com/article/SB10001424052748704694004576020083703574602.html`).

If you use your mobile device strictly for calls and text messages, then you probably only need to worry about what Carrier IQ and your carrier are doing with your personal information. However, if you use apps on your mobile device, your personal information is alive and well and running wild in cyberspace. A commercial appeared on television in the mid-2000s showing the harm done to a high school girl after her friends posted very personal photos of her on a social networking website. The girl endured laughter and suggestive comments from classmates and strangers as she went about her day. The commercial's point was that information posted online lasts forever. To illustrate that point, the commercial portrayed one of the photos as posted on a school's physical bulletin board. No matter how many times the girl tore the photo off the bulletin board, the photo remained. Your personal information suffers the same fate whether you make it available on the Internet or someone else does. Once available on the Internet or to an app, you no longer have control over that information.

Some malware even goes so far as to take control of the device. In doing so, it can cause considerable harm to other devices and the finances of the owner. For example, malware can cause a device to send **short message service (SMS)** text messages to premium rate services, incurring massive bills for the device's owner. The developer of the malware benefits by owning the company providing the service requested by the SMS. Or, the malware can replicate itself through the USB port to infect a computer when the device is attached to it. Once the infected computer is connected to a recognized network, such as a company network, the malware spreads quickly because any firewalls or other protection mechanisms recognize the computer and do not stop it from connecting. As a result, you could unintentionally infect your home or work network without intending to or even knowing about it.

And now the rest of the story

Google (Android) and Apple sell most of the apps through their stores. Why, then, are they not ensuring the apps are secure for users? They claim they do. According to Google, they scan apps using a tool called **Bouncer**. The tool recognizes when an app has been uploaded and immediately analyzes it for known issues. These issues include embedded malware, spyware, Trojans, and malicious behavior. Google also publishes policies for app developers, which include mandatory security requirements. Apps failing Bouncer's testing or found to violate Google's policies are removed from Google Play. However, Google cannot restrict the developers from offering the same apps on third-party app websites (`http://techcrunch.com/2012/11/05/android-malware-surges-despite-googles-efforts-to-bounce-dodgy-apps-off-its-platform-f-secure-ids-51447-unique-samples-in-q3/`). So an app determined as unsafe for your mobile device by Google or Apple may still be available to you for downloading without a warning that it failed the security check.

Apple's track record for dangerous apps is better than Android's; however, it is not perfect, as noted earlier. A flaw was found in Apple's iOS code, which allowed the introduction of malware into Apple apps, and several developers have been able to find loopholes in Apple's security restrictions. In addition, Apple is slow to patch identified security holes, waiting four months to release a patch when 81 vulnerabilities were found in its iOS 5.0.1. During those four months, any number of viruses and Trojans could have been installed on devices running iOS 5.0.1 by hackers taking advantage of the vulnerabilities. A hacker would then have had an open door to steal information from, or even take control of, a compromised device.

Google and Apple are finding it difficult to stay ahead of the malware developers and the challenge is only growing. Some companies are actively finding ways to exploit Android and Apple flaws. Take a look at this job posting, reprinted from a June 2012 Naked Security article:

```
-3 + years of experience with the analysis of host data at rest,
including Microsoft Windows, system internals, and file attributes,
executable file analysis for PE files, including dynamic linked
libraries, File Hashing and Fuzzy File Hashing, including ssdeep,
fciv, and md5deep, forensic analysis of Windows systems, Linux
systems, or mobile devices, Commercial, open source, or GOTS tools
for intrusion detection, including Snort or BroIDS, Packet capture
and evaluation, including tcpdump, ethereal/wireshark, or NOSEHAIR,
Network mapping and discovery, including nmap or TRICKLER, Industry
standard system and network tools, including netcat, netstat,
traceroute, rpcinfo, nbtscan, snmpwalk, or Sysinternals suite,
Exploit development of Microsoft Windows, Exploit development of
Linux, Exploit development of personal computer device and mobile
device operating systems, including Android, Blackberry, iPhone,
and iPad, Software Reverse Engineering, including the use of code
disassemblers, including IDA Pro, debugging unknown code, including
Ollydbg, Analysis of code in memory, including analysis of RAM
snapshots, Windows crash dump files, or Linux kernel dumps
-TS/SCI clearance with a polygraph
-BA or BS degree
```

Refer to http://nakedsecurity.sophos.com/2012/06/29/
apple-mobile-device-security/

So, Google and Apple are striving to make it a safer world for mobile devices? Ad companies are not the only recipients of your information. In the WSJ study, Google received the most data, collecting information from 38 of the apps. Google also has information-collecting wallpaper apps available in its digital store, 80 of them as of the last count. These apps collect and transmit personal information similar to the apps described previously. One in particular, Jackeey Wallpaper, was presented as an app of concern at a Black Hat security conference by Kevin MaHaffey, Lookout's Chief Technology Officer. According to MaHaffey, Jackeey Wallpaper had been downloaded millions of times and transmitted the data collected to a server in China. Google suspended the app after the Black Hat conference (http://www.telegraph.co.uk/technology/google/7918536/Google-Android-apps-collecting-personal-data.html).

Apple also values your personal information. In a patent application filed by Apple, the company indicated its plans to target marketing to people based on the contents of their media libraries and their friends' media libraries. According to the patent, Apple plans to use "known connections on one or more social-networking websites" or "publicly available information or private databases describing purchasing decisions, brand preferences" (http://online.wsj.com/article/SB10001424052748704694004576020083703574602.html). With friends like that...

Who has your data? Round 2...

The **United States Department of Justice (US DoJ)** created a report in 2010, which detailed the length of time each major cell phone company retained records of call and text activities by their customers. The report, *Retention Periods of Major Cellular Providers* (http://www.aclu.org/files/pdfs/freespeech/retention_periods_ of_major_cellular_service_providers.pdf), was followed up by American Civil Liberties Union (ACLU) research in August 2011. The ACLU's goal was to determine how law enforcement agencies used the data retained by the providers. The ACLU found that, of the 230 law enforcement agencies willing to provide information, 217 tracked cell phones with frequencies varying from emergency use only to regularly.

What information about you is available to law enforcement agencies? The answer depends on your cell phone provider. According to the US DoJ report, call and text message detail records are retained for one to seven years, while text message content is retained for zero to 90 days.

How legal is it for police officials to use this information? Is a warrant required before your local police department is allowed to track your movements through your cell phone? The answer is an uncomfortable one for many people. While a GPS tracker placed on a car is considered an unreasonable search by the U.S. Supreme Court, warrants for cell phone tracking are not required in all jurisdictions. However, tracking by cell phone is far more invasive unless the phone is always in the car.

Carriers have determined how to profit from law enforcement agencies' desire to use this readily available information. In fact, some carriers have published price lists to the agencies for various surveillance services. It's not just the carriers playing the cell phone tracking game. The ACLU learned that California state prosecutors provided instructions to local police departments on cloning cell phones to be able to download text messages even when the phones are turned off. In Arizona, local police departments built their own tracking equipment. On the positive side, the Michigan police used cell phone tracking to help locate and save a stabbing victim. Many police departments who responded to the ACLU's questionnaire indicated that they felt the benefit of helping people more than compensated for any legal uncertainties (http://www.nytimes.com/2012/04/01/us/police-tracking-of-cellphones-raises-privacy-fears.html).

One additional fact to keep in mind: you may not be "you" if someone else is using your mobile device. Thus, the tracking information that points to you may in fact be about the person using your device.

You can lose out in at least three ways if law enforcement officers misunderstand or misuse your mobile device information. First, a false profile of you can be developed simply by putting your actual information together incorrectly. Second, the actions of someone you know who used your device can be attributed to you. It would be very difficult to prove actions performed with your device were done by someone else. Third, a false profile of you can be developed by putting together information created by someone masquerading as you as a result of stealing your information from your device.

Who has your data? Round 3...

Retailers also learned about the benefits of knowing where people are based on the location of their cell phones. They developed a technique called location-based marketing, which allows them to determine how to interact with a potential customer based on the customer's location. One type of this marketing technique is called **check-in services**, in which a customer shares their location in exchange for special deals on merchandise and services. The retailer builds a location and purchase profile of the customer and fine-tunes future offers based on that profile (http://www.retailtouchpoints.com/shopper-engagement/1355-forrester-research-highlights-impact-of-location-based-marketing-).

Now, you may be thinking that this sounds like a pretty sweet deal. You can have bargains find you rather than you having to find them. In one sense, that is true. In another sense, what have you paid for that bargain with besides money? You have paid with your personal information compounded into a detailed picture of where you go, what you buy, and what you are willing to spend. Take a few minutes to let that sink in. What is the harm? Once retailers know you are willing to pay $x for an item, they have no incentive to offer the item for less. However, your neighbor two doors down may not be willing to pay as much as you. Retailers will have that information, also. The "bargains" sent to your phone maybe far different from those received by your neighbor. Or, to state it another way, you may pay $200 more for the same television that your neighbor just bought from the same store.

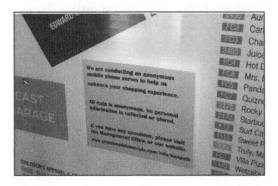

Two shopping malls had a surprise planned for shoppers on Black Friday 2011. Two malls, one in Virginia and one in California, installed antennas throughout their buildings to anonymously track shoppers and analyze their shopping patterns. The antennas picked up cell phone signals and tracked their owners as they shopped. Small signs warned shoppers about the tracking, but provided no escape from the surveillance other than shutting off the phones. According to the company that manages both malls, the information collected did not include the shoppers' names or phone numbers, only their locations (`http://money.cnn.com/2011/11/28/ news/economy/malls_track_shoppers_cell_phones/index.htm`).

The mall management company decided to find more agreeable ways to track shoppers in the future; however, Black Friday 2011 shows that the technology is available.

Who has your data? The final stretch...

A March 2012 news article by *The Telegraph* (`www.telegraph.co.uk`) revealed that Twitter and Path acknowledged copying entire address books from their users' smartphones without the users' consent or knowledge. Add that to retailers tracking you by your mobile device, app developers collecting your personal information, your cell phone provider and their software providers collecting your call and text information, law enforcement agencies mapping where you go, and a comprehensive picture of who you are, what you do, what you own, and where you go begins to emerge.

Let's go back to the persistent cookies, both friendly and malicious. They have been busy collecting information about you while you surf the Web, Internet bank, and shop online. The bad guys who planted the malicious cookies on your machine have already sold your information, probably several times, for a small amount each time. But there is another market, a legal one, which also trades in your information.

Predictive analytics is a data analysis approach in which historical information is studied to gain insights, which are used to make decisions on future actions. The goal for marketers and retailers is to increase profits (`http://www.forbes. com/2010/04/01/analytics-best-buy-technology-data-companies-10- accenture.html`).

Retailers, both physical and online, have learned that they can make money twice on the same customers: the first time by selling products or services, and the second time by selling information about their customers. They do not sell the information to competitors, but rather to companies in other industries or, more likely, to data dealers. The data dealers consolidate data from many sources, combine it into profiles based on predictive analytics, and sell it to interested buyers who use it for targeted marketing. Imagine the value of the analysis after combining all of your calling, texting, banking, and shopping habits. If all of this sounds like science fiction, take a few minutes to review www.digby.com/localpoint/ and www.digby.com/mobile-statistics/, where you will find marketing information such as the following:

DIGBY LOCALPOINT MOBILE PLATFORM

The Digby Localpoint Platform harnesses the power of location to provide retailers and brands with powerful tools for enabling digital, real-time engagement in and around real world locations, all through the consumers' mobile devices.

Localpoint pairs powerful location detection with a contextual engagement engine and best-of-breed notification capabilities to help make branded mobile applications more intelligent, relevant, and engaging.

Localpoint is composed of a lightweight SDK that is easy to embed in your apps for iOS and Android and a web-based console that provides intuitive setup, management, and analytics across your app installbase.

The Value of Right Place, Right Time

Localpoint allows marketers to communicate and engage with customers at precisely the right place and the right time with the right message. Composed of three modules, Localpoint allows brands to achieve their omni-channel goals.

Localpoint Analytics
Attain unprecedented insight into the real-world behaviors of your customer through Localpoint Analytics. Data about your customers' visit patterns and dwell times proves or disproves long-held assumptions about what drives your business, and sheds new light on shopping behavior and location performance.

Localpoint Outreach
Capture the attention of nearby customers and drive foot traffic where you want it with Localpoint Outreach. Timed notifications measure deliveries, opens, and even arrival of the mobile user at the "target" location allowing you to discover campaign success.

Localpoint Venue
Take control of the mobile experience around your place of business with Localpoint Venue, turning customers' own devices into companions that enhance customer satisfaction and influence purchasing behavior while staying in harmony with the real world brand experience you've created.

Also, some more details are seen in the following screenshot:

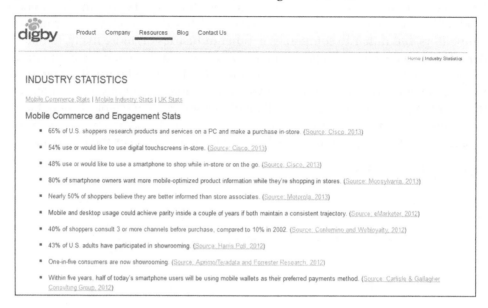

These are actual marketing messages to companies, offering your information consolidated, reformatted, and analyzed to help those companies determine new ways to target ads to your lifestyle and preferences.

From the research gathered by Digby, we can learn of the widespread impact of targeted marketing and shopping via mobile devices. People have become comfortable with this, even somewhat dependent on it. In the U.S., over 74 million people shop using their mobile devices. By 2015, retailers predict that consumers will spend $119 billion on goods and services purchased through their mobile devices.

Of the people surveyed by Digby, 33 percent used a check-in service to share their location with retailers; 64 percent had made at least one mobile purchase after seeing a mobile ad. Twenty-five percent of the respondents stated they do online shopping using their mobile devices exclusively.

Online payments (banking, bill paying) are also growing in popularity. Eighty-two percent of consumers made at least one mobile payment by the end of 2012, with an estimated total paid of over $171.5 billion.

Over one-third of consumers surveyed prefer mobile shopping through an app rather than a web browser. However, apps are better able to collect and transmit data. For the 64 percent mobile shoppers and 82 percent mobile payers, the risk of stolen personal information is very high. The use of mobile devices for many activities, which require personal and sensitive personal information, is expected to continue to grow and grow quickly. The amount of information generated through those activities will grow just as quickly. You may be comfortable with a stranger knowing that much about you and seeking to influence your decisions based on it. Or, you may wish to keep most or all of that information to yourself. Each person has a different privacy comfort level; no one can make that decision for you. Regardless of your comfort level, there are tools to help you control access to your information. The goal is to align how much information you want to share with how much information you are sharing. Before making that decision, there are other things you need to know.

Your data in their hands

Unlike physical theft, data theft is not limited by proximity to the victim. A person in any country is at risk of having data stolen by a thief in any other country. The Internet makes this possible and relatively easy. Not only is the risk of data theft increased by ease, it is also increased by sheer volume when compared to physical theft. There may be a few thieves within driving distance of your home; however, there are an unlimited number of data thieves with access to the Internet.

A thief looking for the right home to rob will search for the building offering the least resistance to intrusion. Data thieves use the same approach. Because mobile devices tend to be protected less than personal computers, they make better targets.

Once thieves have your data, they can sell it to buyers on the black market, once or many times over, or they can use it to steal your identity. They can also do both. In David Crouse's situation, several people bought his information and stole his identity. The options are only limited by preventive and corrective actions you take to stop the use of your data.

How long does your data "live out there" once it is stolen? The surprising answer is forever. Forever is also the length of time data that you intentionally provide survives. Once the data is out there, it cannot be pulled back. It resides in data files on servers owned by many entities including retailers, cell phone carriers, Internet Service Providers, marketing firms, data resellers, law enforcement agencies, employers, and even thieves. Some entities may agree to delete your information if you request it, while others may only remove the portions of data required by law.

Will your money be "too" mobile?

With all the concerns over mobile device malware and data theft, should you even consider using your device for mobile banking or bill paying? The answer is a surprising "Yes, but with precautions." Banks typically have strong security protections, which can work to your advantage. They understand the additional risks inherent in mobile devices. This allows them to implement measures specific to mobile banking, which increase the security of your transactions.

For example, a bank can authenticate you through your phone's unique ID. That would prevent anyone else, using a different device, from accessing your account. A bank can also limit transactions to certain cell tower areas that coincide with your home, office, or school, adding additional security.

Use your bank's app rather than a web browser on your mobile device to ensure use of the highest available protection. You will want to ensure your bank enforces adequate security measures before initiating mobile banking, to be safe (http://www.dailyfinance.com/2012/07/17/why-banking-on-your-smartphone-is-safer-than-using-your-pc/). If you choose to use mobile banking, you should ensure that your bank follows safe mobile banking, including making a safe app available. Not doing so greatly increases the risk that your bank accounts will be compromised.

For paying bills with your mobile device, there are measures you can take to increase security, also. Rather than using Wi-Fi, use your carrier's network when transmitting login credentials and payment information. If the company you are paying has an app, use it to make payments rather than a web browser; the app is likely to be more secure. Ensure you have a mobile security product on your device, including an option to wipe the device remotely if you lose it. Lastly, enable the lock setting on your device to be triggered after a certain number of minutes have passed with no activity; 15 minutes is a good limit (http://www.infosecisland.com/blogview/20669-How-Safe-is-Paying-Online-with-Your-Smart-Phone.html).

Bring your mobile device to work day

A recent poll by an access-management company Courion found that 69 percent of the corporations contacted said their employees use personally-owned mobile devices to connect to the corporate network (http://www.informationweek.com/mobility/security/personal-mobile-devices-still-vex-it/231002676). This practice introduced a whole new security risk to companies through devices over which they have little control. Initially, companies fought the practice but eventually chose to accept the inevitable. Employees won the battle by sheer numbers. "Mobile devices are now accepted as necessary tools for productivity in the enterprise, regardless of how they affect data security. That is the new reality" (www.informationweek.com/news/mobility/security/231002676).

The idea of carrying only one mobile device to fill multiple roles appeals to many employees. One device can handle personal and business calls, personal and business e-mails, report writing, and presentation development. It can also allow the on-the-road employee to keep up with sports scores, bill paying, and the occasional Internet surfing.

Before embracing the single-device practice, there are things to consider. For example, if you use your personal device for work purposes, is your employer allowed to view *all* of the content to determine policy compliance, or only the content that is business-related? Is your employer allowed to use your personal content against you for disciplinary actions? Must you screen what is said even during personal calls and texts? The answers to these questions are not clear-cut.

Many companies are only just beginning to consider and implement personal device policies for the workplace. For those companies that have such a policy in place, it typically includes some or all of the following requirements:

- Sign an agreement to perform certain tasks and allow the company certain rights
- Download and install a security and monitoring app that must remain active
- Authorize the company to limit the websites accessible and/or the apps, which can be downloaded
- Authorize the company to limit the file types and/or type of data, which can be saved to the device
- Automatically lock your device after a set amount of idle time, requiring you to enter a password before using the device again
- Authorize the company to track your device via the phone's **global positioning system (GPS)**

- Authorize the company to remotely wipe all data, or at least all corporate data, from your device in the event that your device is lost or stolen

- Hold the company harmless for the loss or destruction of any personal data

 Refer to `http://www.experts.com/Articles/Risk-With-Using-Personal-Devices-For-Work-By-Robert-Siciliano`, `http://online.wsj.com/article/SB10001424053111904583204576542342696584366.html`, and `http://www.businessweek.com/articles/2012-10-02/the-risks-and-rewards-of-personal-electronics-in-the-workplace` for more information.

One thing to keep in mind: with the GPS feature activated, an employer can track where you are during both work and personal time (`http://www.businessweek.com/articles/2012-10-02/the-risks-and-rewards-of-personal-electronics-in-the-workplace`).

The questions posed earlier regarding your rights are not easily answered and there is no solid guidance for companies to follow. Like most new concepts, it will take time for laws to catch up with life. In the meantime, employers will strive to protect the company and employees will strive to protect themselves. If you choose to use a personal mobile device for work purposes, you will need to determine how much personal information you are willing to make available to your employer beyond that which you gave when you were hired. Without taking this important step, you may be handing over information that could jeopardize your career, even if the information is viewed as innocuous outside the workplace.

Steps you can take to protect yourself

People define privacy in many different ways. Some people are comfortable sharing all the details of their lives in very public social forums, while others prefer to keep a low electronic profile. You can choose how much others may learn about you via your devices, or you can let others make that decision for you. It is important to determine your privacy comfort level before taking steps to protect the information on your mobile device. If you fail to properly define your privacy requirements, you may end up with less protection than you need.

Once you have defined how much protection you need, you can take steps to ensure that protection. Anti-malware and anti-spyware software is now available for mobile devices. It helps to identify software on your mobile device, which may present a threat to you, either through stealing your information or tracking you.

Educating yourself on risks and how to avoid them is a good practice, one that should be followed consistently, such as physical exercise. As Sun Tzu wrote in *The Art of War*:

> *"If you know the enemy and know yourself, you need not fear the result of a hundred battles. If you know yourself but not the enemy, for every victory gained you will also suffer a defeat. If you know neither the enemy nor yourself, you will succumb in every battle."*

Before downloading an app, verify that it is a legitimate one. Malicious developers create knock-offs of real apps to fool people into downloading the fakes. Included in the fake versions are malware, spyware, and/or Trojans that are just waiting to steal your data or take control of your device. Clues to watch for include the developer's name, the number of positive ratings and total ratings, and comments by users. Check more than one source for ratings to ensure a consistency across the sites (`http://blog.trendmicro.com/trendlabs-security-intelligence/checking-the-legitimacy-of-android-apps/`). If any of the information does not seem legitimate, you are better off not downloading the app.

Be aware of what you agree to when you download apps. Once you have agreed to share information, you cannot stop sharing without uninstalling the app. Understand what your phone model shares by default and what your phone's operating system allows apps to do. For example, Android apps may collect the phone's unique identification number without notifying the user. Familiarize yourself with your phone's logs and the meaning of their contents. From the logs, you can learn which apps are transmitting data and notice when log contents change after installing new apps.

The United States Federal Bureau of Investigation (FBI) and the National White Collar Crime Center (NW3C) established a unit called the **Internet Crime Complaint Center (IC3)** to provide a single point of contact for people reporting Internet-related criminal complaints. After researching the complaints, the IC3 refers them to the appropriate law enforcement or regulatory agency. The IC3 also publishes warnings on new threats to people via technology. The unit developed a list of tips to help you protect your mobile device, found at `http://www.fbi.gov/scams-safety/e-scams`, and included in *Appendix C, Tips to Help You Protect Your Mobile Device*.

Summary

In this chapter, we looked at privacy consequences and their triggers related to the use of mobile devices, including:

- Session and persistent cookies, which capture your activities on the Internet

- Malicious software (malware): applications (apps) written to benefit others at your expense

- Apps hidden inside other apps, both innocent and malicious

- Carrier IQ's data collection and transmission app to benefit cell phone providers

- The collection of your personal information through apps, by developers and app distributors including Google and Apple

- Tracking you through you mobile device, and law enforcement agencies' use of that information

- The increased use of mobile devices for shopping, banking, and other activities requiring personal and sensitive personal information

- Targeted marketing and data analytics using your personal information and habits

- The consolidation and sale of your information

- The theft of your personal information and its value to identity thieves

- The permanence of your data once it reaches the Internet

- Lack of clarity regarding your rights if you use your personal mobile device to perform work for an employer

- Steps you can take to protect yourself

The next chapter deals with types of scams and threats related to the use of mobile devices and makes you aware of all the necessary threats that are out there.

4
Mobile and Social – the Threats You Should Know About

Due to the increasing use of smart and mobile phones, the threats against these mobile devices have increased/risen over the last few years. We will take an in-depth look at various scams, phishing, spear phishing, social engineering, Cloud security, viruses, worms, and other threats a user may encounter, and future threats.

In this chapter, we will review various threats that you need to be aware of. They are as follows:

- Scams
- Malware
- SMS spoofing
- Social engineering
- Phishing
- Cloud computing
- Virus

A prediction of the future (and the lottery numbers for next week) scams

Security threats, such as malware, are starting to be manifested on mobile devices, as we are learning that mobile devices are not immune to virus, malware, and other attacks. As PCs are increasingly being replaced by the use of mobile devices, the incidence of new attacks against mobile devices is growing. The user has to take precautions to protect their mobile devices just as they would protect their PC.

One major type of mobile cybercrime is the unsolicited text message that captures personal details. Another type of cybercrime involves an infected phone that sends out an SMS message that results in excess connectivity charges.

Mobile threats are on the rise according to the Symantec Report of 2012; 31 percent of all mobile users have received an SMS from someone that they didn't know. An example is where the user receives an SMS message that includes a link or phone number. This technique is used to install malware onto your mobile device. Also, these techniques are an attempt to hoax you into disclosing personal or private data. In 2012, Symantec released a new cybercrime report. They concluded that countries like Russia, China, and South Africa have the highest cybercrime incidents. Their rate of exploitation ranges from 80 to 92 percent. You can find this report at `http://now-static.norton.com/now/en/pu/images/Promotions/2012/cybercrimeReport/2012_Norton_Cybercrime_Report_Master_FINAL_050912.pdf`.

Malware

The most common type of threat is known as **malware**. It is short for malicious software. Malware is used or created by attackers to disrupt many types of computer operations, collect sensitive information, or gain access to a private mobile device/computer. It includes worms, Trojan horses, computer viruses, spyware, keyloggers and root kits, and other malicious programs.

As mobile malware is increasing at a rapid speed, the U.S. government wants users to be aware of all the dangers. So in October 2012, the FBI issued a warning about mobile malware (`http://www.fbi.gov/sandiego/press-releases/2012/smartphone-users-should-be-aware-of-malware-targeting-mobile-devices-and-the-safety-measures-to-help-avoid-compromise`).

> *The IC3 has been made aware of various malware attacking Android operating systems for mobile devices. Some of the latest known versions of this type of malware are Loozfon and FinFisher. Loozfon hooks its victims by emailing the user with promising links such as: a profitable payday just for sending out email.*

It then plants itself onto the phone when the user clicks on this link. This specific malware will attach itself to the device and start to collect information from your device, including:

- Contact information
- E-mail address
- Phone numbers
- Phone number of the compromised device

On the other hand, a spyware called FinFisher can take over various components of a smartphone. According to IC3, this malware infects the device through a text message and via a phony e-mail link. FinFisher attacks not only Android devices, but also devices running Blackberry, iOS, and Windows.

Various security reports have shown that mobile malware is on the rise. Cyber criminals tend to target Android mobile devices. As a result, Android users are getting an increasing amount of destructive Trojans, mobile botnets, and SMS-sending malware and spyware. Some of these reports include:

- `http://www.symantec.com/security_response/publications/threatreport.jsp`
- `http://pewinternet.org/Commentary/2012/February/Pew-Internet-Mobile.aspx`
- `https://www.lookout.com/resources/reports/mobile-threat-report`

As stated recently in a Pew survey, more than fifty percent of U.S. mobile users are overly suspicious/concerned about their personal information, and have either refused to install apps for this reason or have uninstalled apps.

In other words, the IC3 says:

> *Use the same precautions on your mobile devices as you would on your computer when using the Internet.*

Toll fraud

Since the 1970s and 1980s, hackers have been using a process known as **phreaking**. This trick provides a tone that tells the phone that a control mechanism is being used to manage long-distance calls. Today, the hackers are now using a technique known as **toll fraud**. It's a malware that sends premium-rate SMSs from your device, incurring charges on your phone bill. Some toll fraud malware may trick you into agreeing to murky Terms of Service, while others can send premium text messages without any noticeable indicators. This is also known as **premium-rate SMS malware** or **premium service abuser**.

The following figure shows how toll fraud works, portrayed by Lookout Mobile Security:

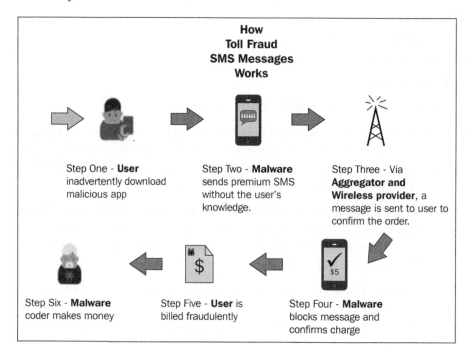

According to VentureBeat, malware developers are after money. The money is in the toll fraud malware. Here is an example from `http://venturebeat.com/2012/09/06/toll-fraud-lookout-mobile/`:

- Remember commercials that say, "Text 666666 to get a new ringtone everyday!"? The normal process includes: Customer texts the number, alerting a collector — working for the ringtone provider — that he/she wants to order daily ringtones.

- Through the collector, the ringtone provider sends a confirmation text message to the customer (or sometimes two depending on that country's regulations) to the customer.

- That customer approves the charges and starts getting ringtones.

- The customer is billed through the wireless carrier.

- The wireless carrier receives payment and sends out the ringtone payment to the provider.

Now, let's look at the steps when your device is infected with the malware known as **FakeInst**:

- The end user downloads a malware application that sends out an SMS message to that same ringtone provider.

- As normal, the ringtone provider sends the confirmation message. In this case, instead of reaching the smartphone owner, the malware blocks this message and sends a fake confirmation message before the user ever knows.

- The malware now places itself between the wireless carrier and the ringtone provider. Pretending to be the collector, the malware extracts the money that was paid through the user's bill.

FakeInst is known to get around antivirus software by identifying itself as new or unique software.

Overall, Android devices are known to be impacted more by malware than iOS. One big reason for this is that Android devices can download applications from almost any location on the Internet. Apple limits its users to downloading applications from the Apple App store.

SMS spoofing

The third most common type of scam is called **SMS spoofing**. SMS spoofing allows a person to change the original mobile phone number or the name (sender ID) where the text message comes from. It is a fairly new technology that uses SMS on mobile phones. Spoofing can be used in both lawful and unlawful ways. Impersonating a company, another person, or a product is an illegal use of spoofing. Some nations have banned it due to concerns about the potential for fraud and abuse, while others may allow it. An example of how SMS spoofing is implemented is as follows: SMS spoofing occurs when the message sender's address information has been manipulated. This is done many times to impersonate a cell phone user who is roaming on a foreign network and sending messages to a home area network. Often, these messages are addressed to users who are outside the home network, which is essentially being "hijacked" to send messages to other networks.

The impacts of this activity include the following:

- The customer's network can receive termination charges caused by the valid delivery of these "bad" messages to interlink partners.

- Customers may criticize about being spammed, or their message content may be sensitive. Interlink partners can cancel the home network unless a correction of these errors is implemented. Once this is done, the phone service may be unable to send messages to these networks.

- There is a great risk that these messages will look like real messages, and real users can be billed for invalid roaming messages that they did not send.

There is a flaw within iPhone that allows SMS spoofing. It is vulnerable to text messaging spoofing, even with the latest beta version, iOS 6. The problem with iPhone is that when the sender specifies a reply-to number this way, the recipient doesn't see the original phone number in the text message. That means there's no way to know whether a text message has been spoofed or not. This opens up the user to other spoofing types of manipulation where the recipient thinks he/she is receiving a message from a trusted source.

According to pod2g (`http://www.pod2g.org/2012/08/never-trust-sms-ios-text-spoofing.html`):

> *In a good implementation of this feature, the receiver would see the original phone number and the reply-to one. On iPhone, when you see the message, it seems to come from the reply-to number, and you loose track of the origin.*

Social engineering

For many attacks to exist, the victim is required to disclose personal information in some way; this is known as social engineering. Hackers are everywhere and they never sleep, whether it might be an SMS text message with an evil intention or a phishing e-mail that is watching every step of yours on your mobile devices.

Whether you're an IT manager protecting employees and corporate systems or you're simply trying to keep your own personal data safe, these threats—some rapidly growing, others still emerging—pose a potential risk.

A good source for a definition of social engineering is `http://en.wikipedia.org/wiki/Social_engineering_(security)`.

Social engineering is committing an act of manipulating people into executing actions or disclosing confidential information, such as an ID and password or bank account, credit card, or social security number. There are two forms of social engineering: one is phishing and the other is spear phishing, where persons represent themselves as trustworthy entities in an electronic communication.

Phishing

Phishing is the fraudulent act of attempting to capture personal-sensitive information by masquerading through a trustworthy/legitimate source e-mail. These types of attacks can utilize social engineering tactics. Phishing e-mails may include links leading to websites that are infected with malware. Using this trust, they then attempt to acquire sensitive information such as usernames, account passwords, credit card data, and sensitive corporate information. These attacks are pretty broad-based, typically involving spam e-mail or other communications distributed to many people. An example is the kind of e-mail requesting "verification" of information while warning of some dire consequence if it is not provided. Be particularly wary of unsolicited communications. It is better to type the URL out directly than copy and paste it.

Here is an example:

A user receives an e-mail from their bank, asking them to verify their account information such as username and password. The user clicks on the link where they enter their username and password.

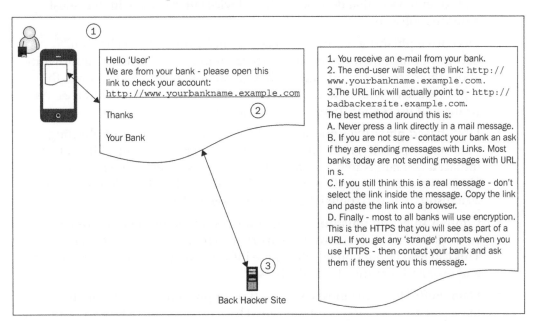

Here is another example:

If the Groupon application on the iPhone wants to share something on Facebook, the program typically pops up a window that invites the user to sign into that website. But, there's usually no way to be sure that the login site is legitimate and that the phone's owner is really sending their username and password to Facebook. Users are manipulated this way; therefore, you should never enter any sensitive information and always use extra caution.

Overall, it is difficult for mobile phone users to distinguish real websites from fake ones. The smaller screens on mobile phones don't help this identification process.

Types of phishing

There are a variety of attack types; let's review a few:

- **Malware-based phishing**: This type of phishing involves running malicious software on users' devices. It is easy to introduce malware as a downloadable file on a website or an e-mail. One easy target is smaller companies and/or end users that don't keep their devices up to date with the latest antivirus software.

- **Deceptive phishing**: Using e-mail as a primary delivery mechanism, deceptive phishing uses e-mail to trick the end user into sharing information about their account information. Though not totally limited to e-mail, this type of trickery will try to tell you that you have fictitious account fees. As a result, end users share personal information.

- **DNS-based phishing (pharming)**: This is an advanced type of phishing. Pharming, specially, is the modification of a system host's file. This can also impact a Domain Name System (DNS). This is as dangerous as it sounds. Hackers are messing with a corporate host file and/or the DNS system and as a result, they can route URLs to the hacker's sites.

- **Content Injection phishing**: Content Injection is where a hacker replaces some part of a legitimate website in order to redirect the user to a fake site. This can also be a modified site where information is in effect stolen from the end user and sent directly to the hacker.

- **Data theft**: This is the most common type of phishing. PCs that are not well managed are easy targets for hackers. These types of PCs are not authorized PCs, or PCs that don't have all of the needed virus scanning software installed. These unsecure PCs can be used to access corporate servers and steal a business's intellectual data.

- **Search engine phishing**: This phishing type provides a user with very sophisticated, attractive, and legitimate sounding genuine offers that shows up in the proper index of the search engine. Hackers create these searchable websites. These websites show up during the normal course of a user searching for products or services and are tricked into giving up their sensitive information. A prime example of this type of scam is where scammers set up false banking sites with lower credit rates or better interest rates for mortgages or personal loans. Victims are lured to these sites in order to make more interest or even save themselves from interest charges. The victim is encouraged to give up their personal information.

Other types of attacks include:

- **System reconfiguration attacks**: This type of attack will modify configuration settings on a user's desktop. Once these malicious settings have been installed, hackers can control devices.

- **Keyloggers and screenloggers**: This is a very old type of attack. Keyloggers have been around for a long time. This attack will actually track each of the keys pushed and then send that data out to the hackers' servers.

Spear phishing

Now that we have introduced you to phishing, let's now talk about **spear phishing**. Spear phishing is another method that can be used to steal your identity. Spear phishing targets individuals. This type of attack is customized to one person at a time. This type of attack is on the rise mostly on mobile devices. Mobile devices are being used more and more for corporate access. This attack exposes not only the end user, but also the corporation's network they connect to. Spear phishing uses data that is directly from an end user; for example, social media information or e-mail. These are very personalized attacks.

BYOD devices today are hooked into the corporate network. This access includes access not only to the end user's information, but also corporate information, like a corporate directory of users. If the corporate directory is compromised, hackers now have a larger set of end users they can attack.

How spear phishing works

Spear phishing normally uses e-mail as the delivery mechanism. One example includes an e-mail that has a URL (hyperlink) that points to a fake website. The fake website will collect personal information once it is accessed. In many cases a file is attached. This can be very convincing, as the source message looks to be real. The user launches the attachment and then executes the malware that can destroy the device, or in this example, will extract personal information from the device and send it directly to the hacker.

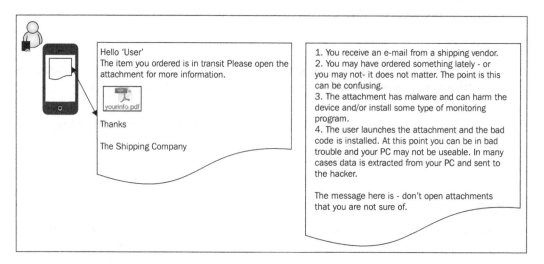

Other examples

Let's have a look at some examples of spear phishing.

Receiving e-mails from a "friend"

The spear phisher grows vigorously by using familiarity. Cyber criminals know your first and last name, your e-mail address, and at least a little something personal about yourself. The e-mail message salutation is very likely to be personalized: "Hi Steve" instead of "Dear Sir/Madam." The e-mail may make reference to a "mutual/common friend", to a recent search you've made about a product or an item, or a recent online purchase you've made. Because the e-mail sender's information is from someone you are very familiar with, you may be less vigilant and provide them with any information they ask for. With an urgent request for action, you may be tempted to act before thinking, especially when it's a company you frequently access that is asking.

Using your web presence against you

Do you know you are becoming a target for spear phishing? The information you are providing on the Internet from your PC or a smartphone can make you a target. For example, they might scan social networking sites, find your e-mail address, your page, a recent post by you telling friends about the cool new laptop or a tablet you bought at an online retail site, and your friends list. By using this information, a spear phisher could pose as a friend, send you an e-mail, and ask you for personal information or a password to your photo page. If you respond with the password, the phishers will try that password and many combinations of it in order to try to access your personal accounts on that online shopping site you mentioned. If they find the right one, they'll use it to run up a nice big expensive tab for you; or the spear phisher might pose as somebody from the online retailer by using the same information and ask you to reset your password, or re-verify your credit card number. If you do this, you'll mess up your financial information and cause yourself harm.

Keeping your secrets secret

Are you safe and is your information safe? It really depends in part on you being careful. Check your online presence with your names. Check your social networking threads. Be aware of your information and how much is out there about you that could be pieced together for someone to scam you. Also, the data you put on the Internet "stays on the Internet". Some of this information can include:

- Your name.
- E-mail address.
- Friends' names.
- Your friends' e-mail addresses.
- Are you on, for example, any of the popular social networking sites?
- Be sure and look at your daily posts on various social networking sites.
- Beware of giving too much information on social sites. Don't over share.
- Be proactive and don't reveal too much.
- Is there anything you don't want a scammer to know?
- Have you posted something on a friend's page that might reveal too much?

Be sure to ask yourself all these questions. Google your name and be aware. Refer to the following example screenshot:

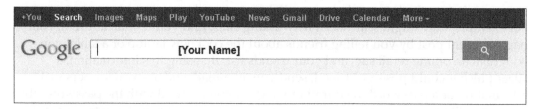

Passwords that work

A lot of people have common passwords. They use the same password on multiple sites and services, use "easily guessed passwords", or both. Rethink about all of your passwords. Do you use just one or easy to figure out variations on just one? If you do either, you shouldn't, because you're making yourself a target for a scammer to get access to your sensitive financial information. Every password for every site you visit should be different, really unique. Random letters, upper or lower cases, and numbers work best. Change them frequently, every two to three months. Your Internet security software and operating system can help you keep track of your passwords.

Here is a common technique that hackers use to find your passwords:

Hackers will obtain information about you: your name, your e-mail, or other personal information. Also, the hacker will find where your bank is and/or what corporate sites you use. Word lists are very common on the Internet; hackers will obtain these lists as a starting point. Hackers will write simple code to create password lists. Each password will be modified so it can be used as an attack against your websites; for example, e-mail.

Passwords will be created using a simple algorithm: [Base word] & [character change] & [Character add].

For example, Base words - password, or your last name.

Formula, "password" & [change the letter a to @] & [add a "01"].

This creates the following potential passwords:

- p@ssword01
- p@ssword02
- p@ssword03
- p@ssword04
- p@ssword05

- p@ssword06

- p@ssword07

- p@ssword08

- p@ssword09

Follow the Johnson example: `"johnson"` & `[change the letter 's' to $]` & `[add a "01" to "09"]`.

- John$on01

- John$on02

- John$on03

- John$on04

- John$on05

- John$on06

- John$on07

- John$on08

- John$on09

Based on the preceding example, you can see why you need more complex passwords and why passwords should be changed on a regular basis. Now with personal information extracted from you (or even via a search engine), hackers will attack your account with the same username (`mike.johnson@example.com`) and then each of the passwords created. This is an automated process and has a high success rate. Yes, this can take a while, but hackers will have used thousands of PCs they would have gotten control of via other techniques. Review this article to see how powerful this technique is: `http://arstechnica.com/security/2012/12/25-gpu-cluster-cracks-every-standard-windows-password-in-6-hours/`.

Patches, updates, and security software

Always keep your software patches up to date. When you get notices from software vendors to update your software, never ignore these notifications, just do it. Most operating system and browser updates include security patches. Sometimes, it only takes your name and e-mail address for a hacker to slip through a security hole into your system. And it almost goes without saying, you should be protected by Internet security software.

Be vigilant

Always be vigilant and proactive. If a "friend" e-mails and asks for a password or other information, call or e-mail (in a separate email) that friend and ask them to verify that they really contacted you. As we have noted before you need to check with your vendor (bank or other) and make sure these messages are valid. Keep in mind that most legitimate businesses will never e-mail you asking for passwords or account numbers. This may not sound fair, but it is up to you to be alert. If in doubt, don't select the link that is in the e-mail. Now regarding texting, please don't send personal information via text; this is just asking for trouble.

Cloud computing security

Cloud computing is a service that is provided on the Internet using shared computing resources such as hardware and software. These services are implemented, managed, and in many cases provide a controlled secure environment for customers. These services are available to users when requested via the Internet from a Cloud computing provider's servers, including hardware, software, and in many cases networking. This computing service does not use a company's own servers. Also, there are hybrid solutions that are provided to customers that can be used as transition services and/or a set of partial services that a customer can purchase. It is designed to provide users easy access to applications, shared resources, and services managed by the Cloud service provider. Some examples of Cloud services are online data storage, backup solutions, web-based e-mail services, hosted office suites, and document collaboration services. There are many public Cloud services that can be used to create, store, back up, and share data, including Google Docs, Dropbox, Microsoft 365 Apps, Carbonite, Apple iCloud, and SlideShare. Most likely, most of you out there have already used some forms of Cloud computing. If you have any kind of web-based e-mail service like Gmail, Yahoo! Mail, or Hotmail, you have some experience with Cloud computing. The software and storage is stored in your online account and it does not exist on your computer.

How it works

When speaking about cloud computing architecture, it's useful to separate it into three levels: the frontend, the network layer, and the backend. All these ends are connected through a network, usually the Internet. The frontend is the user side of the computer or a mobile device, while the backend is the Cloud section of the system.

The following figure shows a sample Cloud solution:

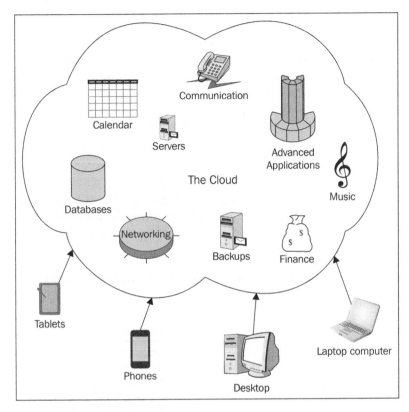

Recently, cloud computing has picked up speed and is transforming the Internet computing infrastructure. Also, mobile applications and mobile devices have developed rapidly. Mobile devices can use the Cloud for data processing, storage, and other intensive processing operations. Mobile Cloud computing refers to the availability of Cloud services in a mobile environment. It is a combination of the mobile network and Cloud computing, thereby providing optimal services for mobile users. Cloud computing exists when tasks and data are kept on the Internet rather than on individual mobile devices, providing on-demand access. Applications run on a remote server and are then sent to the user.

Since mobile Cloud computing users are growing, the issue of Cloud security comes into picture. Cloud security threats comes in all shapes and sizes. Securing a mobile Cloud computing user's privacy and integrity of data or applications is one of the key issues most Cloud providers are giving attention too. Although mobile Cloud computing is a combination of mobile networks and Cloud computing, the security risks are divided into two areas: the mobile network user's security and Cloud security.

The mobile user's security

Some of the greatest concerns for mobile devices include:

- **Security**: The idea of a company handing over important data to another company for computing services causes concern for some people. Users are very skeptical to take advantage of the Cloud computing system. The concern revolves around the security risks inherent with the use of mobile applications. The simplest ways to detect security threats will be installing and running through software and antivirus programs on their mobile devices.

- **Privacy**: Providing private personal information such as indicating your current location and user's important information creates scenarios for privacy issues. For example, the use of **location-based services (LBS)** provided by **Global Positioning System (GPS)** devices could expose the user's privacy to a threat. Threats could be minimized through selecting and analyzing the enterprise's needs and requiring only specified services to be acquired and moved to the Cloud.

The following table shows some of the mobile security features that are manifested between iOS and Android:

Features	iOS	Android
Methods of application distribution	By default, the iOS applications can only be downloaded through the Apple App store.	Android has larger distribution channels. More downloadable places are available to download applications from. Inadvertently, this makes it a higher risk.
Weaknesses	Every iOS device running on lower than version 4.3.5 is vulnerable to a flaw called SSL MITM, which hackers can exploit easily.	Millions of Android phones that are still under contract cannot be updated to the latest version of the Android OS.
SandBox	Both iOS 5 and Android 4.0 Ice Cream Sandwich use sandboxing to isolate applications from each other and from sensitive operating system features.	Both iOS 5 and Android 4.0 Ice Cream Sandwich use sandboxing to isolate applications from each other and from sensitive operating system features.
Remote wipe	Both platforms support remote wipe.	Both platforms support remote wipe.

Features	iOS	Android
Jailbreak or rooting	If a device owner chooses to jailbreak their phone, he/she can be more vulnerable to malware.	If a device owner chooses to root their phone, he/she can be more vulnerable to malware.
Malware	iPhone jailbreak exploits security holes that may also be exploited by hackers.	The lack of review has led to an increasing volume of Android specific malware.

 Android application marketplace has limited security implementation via limited inspection. In general, Google chose to allow nearly any application hosted on the marketplace for users to download.

Even with improved security over traditional desktop-based operating systems, both iOS and Android are still vulnerable to many existing categories of attacks.

Cloud security

The following list shows several cloud security/issues that users should be aware of:

- **Data location**: Cloud data can be hosted most anywhere. Your personal data and/or corporate data can be hosted on a server anywhere connected to the Internet. The data can be in any city or country. Before you host your data, or corporate data, be sure to learn about security hosting laws. One example is the Safe Harbor Act: http://export.gov/safeharbor/eu/eg_main_018476.asp.

- **Data segregation**: This refers to storage of Cloud data stored in a shared architecture alongside others users data. In some cases, data can be encrypted within the Cloud. Also, data can be segregated within the cloud. Be sure to check with your provider and see how they manage your data in the Cloud.

- **Privileged user access**: When you host your data outside your own computer, someone will have access to that data. Make sure you obtain information about the people who manage this data and verify what processes they use to keep your data safe.

- **Security compliance**: At the end of the day, you are responsible for the security of your data, even if the data is hosted by a third party. Again, check with your service provider and ask how your data is managed.

- **Disaster recovery (DR)**: Disaster recovery is the process where data is hosted in several locations. If the primary site shuts down and/or is destroyed, a secondary site can bring your data back online. Contact your provider and ask about the service levels they use on hosting your data. If you are really interested in DR, check out NISSST800-34 (`http://csrc.nist.gov/publications/nistpubs/800-34-rev1/sp800-34-rev1_errata-Nov11-2010.pdf`). Contact your service provider and ask them how long it takes to bring your secondary data source online for your access.

Virus/worms/others

We, as mobile device users, think that we are not capable of getting infected by any kind of viruses on our mobile devices. But, the truth is, we are vulnerable to all kinds of threats. Anyone who has any kind of mobile device are at risk of getting a virus if you are not careful or do not protect yourself. Some of the most common notable mobile viruses, Trojans, and worms are:

- **Skulls**: This Trojan virus replaces all phone desktop icons with images of a skull and the device becomes useless.

- **ZitMo**: The ZitMo malware targets users' online banking information. Once this malware is installed, the bad software will forward all incoming SMS messages to a command and control center. Once this data has been shared with the hackers, they will use that data to attack your banking accounts.

- **DroidKungFu**: This is a powerful Trojan for Android applications that obtains manager/master privileges on your device. This virus collects and sends the data to a remote server.

- **Zeus**: Another Trojan horse that steals banking information. This malware is executed by a process known as man-in-the-browser keystroke logging. Zeus is spread mainly through drive-by downloads and phishing schemes.

- **CommWarrior**: This is one of the first worms that uses **Multimedia Messaging Service** (**MMS**) in order to spread to other devices.

- **SpyEye**: This injects new fields into a web page. This technique is called HTML injection. It results in a request for data from users trying to use their banking websites. This malware can include login prompts and password requests. Once hackers have this data, they can access your bank accounts.

- **Ikee**: This particular malware only works on phones that are jailbroken. This book discusses the risk with jailbreaking and this is one of the big ones.

- **Gingermaster**: This malware was created for the Android platform. This particular malware spreads by installing an application that contains a hidden set of code that runs in the background on the device. This virus exploits a specific release of the Android software, Gingerbread 2.3. The result is that the malware creates a service that steals information from the targeted device.

Future threats

In the short history of mobile devices, one of the areas that has received a lot of attention is BYOD. Bringing your own device to work is not only a significant part of recent history, but will be a part of our near future. Looking at the future, we judge that we will see more and more malware for mobile devices. Overall, we expect to see more of the following:

- Malware that takes advantage of your location via the Global Positioning System (GPS). You use this as part of your map programs, and vendors are also starting to use GPS to help identify customers as they walk in their door. More and more applications are using GPS.

- Hackers will take data from your device and use it for phishing and social engineering. This is why it is so important for you to protect your personal information. It is easy for hackers to violate your privacy and then use your data against you.

- We also predict more applications that look to be legitimate, but in reality are a platform for hackers to attack you.

- More use of SMS and other messages to deliver infected payloads of malware.

- We will also see more malware that is customized to you.

- As more mobile devices are infected, a greater number of corporate networks will be infected. This will be a big issue for corporate administrators.

Steps you can take to protect yourself

If you are using a smartphone, tablet, or any other mobile device, follow these guidelines to protect yourself:

- Always use extra caution and install only approved applications available through your vendor's official application store.

  Also, be sure to check any feedback from the download site. This can clue you into any known issues.

- Do not jailbreak or root your smartphone or tablet computer, as this disables critical security features in the device's operating system.

- Before using Wi-Fi hotspot functionality, including smartphones and portable hotspot devices, WPA2 Wi-Fi encryption security must be enabled and configured with a strong password to prevent unauthorized access to the Wi-Fi network created by the device.

- Use a password/pin that is difficult for others to guess.

  There is an advanced feature that you can use, known as **two-factor authentication**. Ask your vendor/application provider if they support this.

- Change your phone and voicemail password often. One suggestion is at least every three months. Also, make sure you don't use any "default" passwords.

- As you don't know who is lurking around or watching you, don't provide too much personal information online; this includes pictures.

- Don't view sensitive personal information on public Wi-Fi.

- It is very important for you to sign out of your applications when you are done.

- Check your Twitter/Facebook privacy settings.

- Don't reveal too much on social media sites and be discrete.

- Lock down your security on your mobile device.

- Avoid clicking e-mail links.

- Use mobile security software; for example, Lookout.

- Use mobile device management software.

- Install OS updates and security hotfixes as soon as it is available for download to ensure your mobile device firmware is up to date.

Summing it up

Mobile security threats are on the rise, and this trend is destined to grow as more people turn to using any kind of mobile device, whether smartphone or tablet, in their day-to-day lives. The best approach for any device user is to practice mobile security and be aware of the various issues and risks. Take all the necessary safety precautions or measures to protect yourself against hackers taking control of your mobile devices.

Summary

In this chapter, we looked at various types of scams and threats related to the use of mobile devices. The next chapter will show you the specifics on how to protect yourself from the various threats identified. We provided ways of recognizing or being aware of all the necessary threats that are out there, including the following details:

- Scams or threats have been increasing in the last four to five years.

- Malicious software (malware) written to benefit others at your expense.

- Toll fraud sends premium-rate SMS from your device, incurring charges on your phone bill.

- SMS spoofing allows a person to change sender's mobile number, which is the ID and also the name where the text messages come from.

- The increased use of mobile devices for shopping, banking, and other activities requiring personal and sensitive personal information.

- Social engineering and how it impacts mobile devices, divulging sensitive confidential information, and also manipulating users into performing actions.

- A fraudulent act of attempting to capture personal sensitive information by masquerading through a trustworthy/legitimate source e-mail.

- Several known types of phishing acts.

- Spear phishing is the new black mark in identity theft. It is important for you to recognize the known types of spear phishing.

- Recognizing and understanding what Cloud computing is.

- Knowing and understanding Cloud security risks.

- Mobile security is divided into two areas: mobile user's security and Cloud security.

- Android devices have higher security risk factors than iOS devices.

- Recognizing and understanding known viruses and worms.

- The permanence of your data once it reaches the Internet.

- Future threats to be aware of.

- Steps you can take to protect yourself.

Now that we have introduced you to mobile device threats, the next chapter will talk about a concept that many people are not aware of, **Mobile Device Management (MDM)**, which is used by many companies today.

5

Protecting Your Mobile Devices

As you have learned from previous chapters, there is a staggering variety of methods that hackers can use to access your smartphone device without your permission. In this chapter, we will discuss the steps you can take to reduce the likelihood that your device will be hacked. We will also discuss the steps you can take in the event that you become the victim of an attack. You will learn about the following:

- What identification numbers are used to identify your smartphone
- Jailbreaking and rooting
- The importance of strong passwords
- Device encryption and antivirus
- How to manage a compromised device
- How you can protect yourself and your device, including protecting

Identifying your phone – the numbers that set your device apart

There are numerous identifiers for each device and network. A **subscriber identity module (SIM)** is an integrated circuit chip that stores the various identification numbers used by a mobile device. The SIM circuit is normally installed into a removable "SIM card".

These may be considered in much the same way as an IP number on a personal computer; they assist carriers in distinguishing one device from another and, therefore, also assist in a carrier's efforts to track and monitor each device. The following are definitions for a few of these identifiers. As a user, these will be most important to you in the event that your device is hacked; you will be able to understand these terms in your efforts to recover or repair your device.

- **IMEI** – the **International Mobile Station Equipment Identity** number is a unique identifier, which is assigned to many mobile devices, from tablets to smartphones. In some countries, such as the United Kingdom and Australia, these numbers are used as a method of blocking stolen devices from accessing cellular networks. Some cellular carriers in the United States have recently begun to implement this sort of blocking feature as well, though the practice is still not widely in use.

- **ICCID** – the **Integrated Circuit Card Identifier** is a unique identifier attached to each SIM within every cell phone. Just as an IMEI may be used to track and identify a cell phone, an ICCID may be used to track a particular SIM card. Using the ICCID and a formula, it is possible to deduce a SIM card's IMSI number.

- **IMSI** – an **International Mobile Subscriber Identity** number is a 15-digit number, which contains network identifying information, such as a mobile country code and mobile network code. Using the IMSI, it is possible to significantly narrow the geographical location of a SIM card.

 You would only be able to identify the name and the location of the original SIM issuer, that is, Vodafone, UK or AT&T, USA. If a user was roaming in a different country, obviously the location would be incorrect.

- **eCID** – an **Electronic Chip Identifier** is a unique number, which is primarily used by Apple to recognize its products. This number is often used by individuals interested in *jailbreaking* Apple products.

- **MEID** – the **mobile equipment identifier** is a globally unique number identifying a specific physical piece of CDMA mobile equipment.

These numbers, when taken in concern, form the *identity* of your smartphone device. This is how cell phone carriers and your device's manufacturer will recognize your device in the event that you report it stolen or in the event that you violate the terms of agreement. In fact, efforts at jailbreaking devices often involve an individual's ability to subvert this identification process.

An easy method to check the numbers on your iPhone is the **iPhone Configurator**. You can find this at `http://support.apple.com/kb/dl1466`.

Take a look at the following screenshot; this is an example of the iPhone configuration utility:

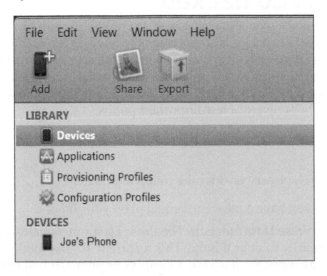

 The iPhone Configuration Utility can also be found in the XCode Organizer.

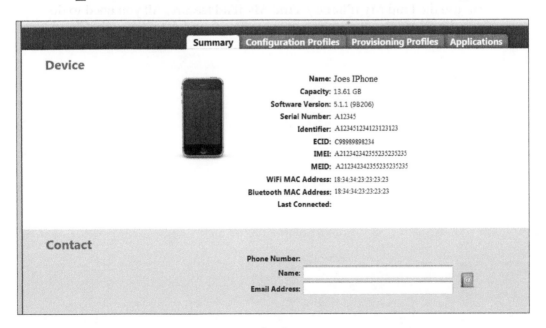

Preventative measures – how to reduce the likelihood that your device will be hacked

While it may sometimes seem otherwise, you are not helpless in protecting your device against potential attacks. Hackers rely on a few specific points of access in their attempts to hack your device; user ID entry, data encryption, and applications. By taking some simple steps to strengthen these potential access points, you can reduce the likelihood that hackers will be successful in their attempts at hacking your smartphone. Let's review a few important points.

iPhone

For an iPhone device, please consider the following points:

- Make sure you have a password enabled on your iPhone.

- Enable the **Erase Data** function. The Erase Data functionality adds another layer of security to your iPhone. This feature will erase all data after 10 failed passcode attempts. So, if a hacker steals your phone, it will remove all data after 10 unsuccessful attempted on the password. To enable this, you need to set **Erase Data** to **ON** in the **Passcode Lock** screen.

- **Find my iPhone** – if you ever lose or misplace your iPhone or iPad, you can use the **Find My iPhone / Find My iPad** feature. All you need to do is to download the application on your device and get it through iCloud (icloud.com).

- **Encrypted Backup** – the **Encrypt Backup** setting is found in iTunes. This setting applies to the new iCloud service in iOS 5. Once enabled, this setting will ensure that the backup of your device is encrypted.

Android

For an Android device, please consider the following points:

- Enable lock screens – you can find this under the **Settings | Security settings**
- Disable USB debugging – you will find this under the **Settings | USB debugging** section
- Enable full disk encryption – this is found in the **Settings | Security** section
- Be sure and only use official application stores

- **Screen lock** – make sure you have enabled a screen lock on your phone, that way it will automatically lock the phone after it is idle for a few minutes

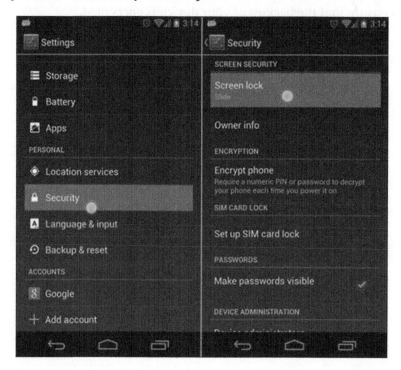

For any device
Make sure that you have the latest OS installed.

Think twice before jailbreaking or rooting

Jailbreaking is the practice of cracking your own device. Jailbreaking in effect bypasses the limitations and restrictions that are put in place by the manufacturer that protect the device. By bypassing these restrictions, basically someone tries to install applications that are not compliant with the supporting applications for either Apple and/or Android. The practice can also unlock some of the restrictions that a specific telecommunications carrier may place on your device.

Rooting, on the other hand, pertains to Android devices. While Apple is stricter about application installation, some Android users feel it necessary to overcome what they feel are operating system limitations. The practice gives them the ability to control all functions on their device. In general, jailbreaking will violate the terms and conditions on the device and can violate your support and/or warranty.

It has been estimated by Cyndia that only **10 percent** of smartphones are now jailbroken or rooted. There are many reasons why this may be such a low number, not the least of which is the concern that doing this might turn the device into a very expensive and useless brick. The other may be that many providers have made more services available for the phones and that many more applications have been developed to meet the demand the public has.

Unfortunately, both practices compromise the device and may allow the *leakage* of passwords, location information, and other personal information that should not be made public. It also greatly increases the likelihood that insecure channels are created and make available a direct pathway on your device to allow malware and other malicious software to be loaded onto your device without your knowledge. The best practice is to not be tempted by the promised benefits. Contacting your provider regarding desired additions to your device may appear costly, but doing it yourself through other channels could be catastrophic. The temporary benefits could be far from acceptable but the consequences may be overwhelming.

Safety in numbers – passwords and user IDs

Today, it seems as though every service requires a user ID and password. We need them to access our bank accounts, our social networking accounts, our employee accounts, and much more. Because of the bewildering variety of account IDs, which we must manage, it can be tempting to re-use the same usernames, IDs, or passwords for multiple accounts. After all, this would reduce the likelihood that we might forget our user ID or password. According to a recent survey on ZDNet, about 60 percent of users admit to using the same password for multiple online accounts (http://www.zdnet.com/blog/security/survey-60-percent-of-users-use-the-same-password-across-more-than-one-of-their-online-accounts/9489).

Management of passwords can be a bit of a challenge. This can also be an issue with your corporate network and servers. The authors have worked with many large companies and we have found that, in some cases, the calls to a specific help desk can overload a help desk with just password changes. These changes are due to lost and/or forgotten passwords. Also, the authors find that these calls can be in excess of 60 percent of all calls into a help desk.

Hackers often target user ID and password information because of the prominence of duplicated login information. If a hacker can obtain the login information for one account, they can use that information to access some of that same user's other accounts. Hackers do not always obtain a user's login information by targeting a specific user's account; they are sometimes able to access a large database of user accounts by targeting a company's database. As of this writing, the most recent notable attack of this nature was the January 2012 hack of Twitter's user database. As many as 250,000 user accounts were compromised in the attack.

What this means for you, as a user, is that you should not feel secure if you utilize a complex password and user ID which, in your opinion, would be difficult for a prospective hacker to "crack". In the event that your account information was compromised as part of one of these large-scale attacks, the complexity of your login information would be insignificant if you have consistently used the same username and password for every one of your accounts.

Hackers can obtain your login information in numerous ways, many of which have been mentioned in prior chapters; large-scale attacks on companies, phishing scams, SMS spoofing, and so on. Because of the variety of methods available to hackers, you should also use numerous methods to reduce the damage a hacker can do once they have your login information. One issue is where a website/service can e-mail users their password in plain text; this shows the data is not being stored using one way cryptographic storage in their database. If the vendor can decrypt it to send it in plain text, so can the hacker.

Using strong passwords

The first place to start is to create *strong* passwords; these are passwords that are difficult for a hacker to guess.

You should not use any personal information. Consider how easily a hacker might be able to obtain this sort of personal information; much of it can be found through online searches or through browsing social networking accounts. If you decided to use personal information to form your password or user ID, a hacker may be able to deduce what it is based on what he or she knows about you personally or from information you have posted online.

You can negate this possibility by ensuring that your passwords do not contain any personally identifying information. Do not use, for example, your pet's name or your child's birth date as the basis for your passwords. Instead, your passwords and user IDs should be as nonspecific as possible. Logically consistent formulations such as nouns or number patterns should be avoided.

Longer and varied passwords

Shorter passwords and user IDs are easier to crack because of their simplicity. According to a recent study by Carnegie Mellon, the length of a password is the most important variable that differentiates strong passwords from the weak. According to the researchers, strong passwords contain at least eight characters, with the strength of the password increasing with each additional character. In other words, the longer the password is, the better it is for you (`http://usatoday30.usatoday.com/tech/news/story/2012-07-28/techlicious-password-security/56540586/1`).

Long and nonsensical passwords are stronger than logically consistent and short passwords because hackers do not always attempt to personally deduce targeted account information. Often, hackers will utilize a type of program known as a **password cracker** or **password attacker**. These programs use algorithms based on common password patterns to *guess* a user's login information. Given enough time, these programs can crack many seemingly impregnable passwords.

One example of a long password is:

Start with: My cat has a hat.

Your password is:

myC@1hasah0T

As a user, your best method of protecting against these sorts of programs is by lengthening your password and ensuring it is nonsensical. Making a password nonsensical means that your password contains no recognizable patterns; no words, no numerical patterns, and no consistency such as lowercase-to-uppercase variation. To test the effectiveness of a password and to obtain an estimate on the amount of time it might take to crack a password, you can use free online services such as **passfault** (`https://passfault.appspot.com/password_strength.html`) or **password meter** (`http://www.passwordmeter.com/`). Entering the word **Cat** on passfault, for example, reveals an estimated time to crack of less than one day. Alternately, passfault estimates **49eXp1nfL3** with a time of one century, two decades. While not an exact measure of password strength, these sorts of services can be helpful in recognizing a particular password's weaknesses.

In addition to creating a strong password, you should also develop different passwords and user IDs for each of your accounts. Do not use the same login information for numerous accounts, however convenient this may seem. While reusing the same login information can reduce the hassle of needing to remember multiple passwords and login IDs, this practice can be significantly more inconvenient in the event that your login information for one account is hacked.

Now, let's be realistic. You have the device to make your life easier. You use it daily and cannot walk around with a written card or sticky note to remind you of what *every* user ID and password actually is. The keyboard is less than friendly on mobile devices and complex usernames and passwords often sound like a good idea, but in ease of use on the device the good practice slides easily into dis-use. While it would be a simple task for the hacker to enter the user information obtained from one account into another. That is not what you are thinking about as you create a password or user ID.

There are various apps available for Android, iOS, and Blackberry devices to help you. They are available from the app store associated with your device platform and can make things simpler. Some are available free and others are paid apps. But a good rule of thumb for creating a new user ID could be something that makes sense to you. If you happen to like American Racing Breed horses and the letters A. R. B. are not your initials try something like this — you are creating a new online banking account. For the username, you key in ARB and the name of the bank with a number – ARB2chase or arb2chase. That will be much different than your e-mail address (hopefully) or anything associated with your name. Re-use those same first characters if need be or a variation of them.

One caveat; if people know you love race horses and you are constantly talking about it in one social media forum or another. Do not use it. Make sure that you choose something that only you know about you. Make sure you do not share the information and do not start posting pictures of horses on Facebook.

Passwords can be another matter. Those same keyboard limitations on a device make it difficult to key them in correctly and you could possibly be locked out of your account. If you are using your mobile device as your primary means to access an account, for example, your app store account — look at your keyboard and try to decide what would be the easiest phrase that you know combined with numbers. Do not replace the letter *O* with a zero or the letter *I* with the number one; that is much too obvious. So, let's say you opened the Chase account we previously discussed to buy stocks. Consider using the phrase buystocks as the password but with some significant changes. By choosing the numbers above certain letters, buystocks can become **b87s6ocks** in one variation. Just to clarify, the *8* is the number above the letter *U* on a normal QWERTY keyboard and the number *7* is the number above the *Y*, just as the *6* is above the *T*. By linking the password to what your purpose is on this site and substituting numbers in place of letters, you have created a more secure environment than if you used your email address or last name and repeated the same password as you did for everything else. By developing numerous passwords and user IDs, you can effectively contain the potential damage in the event that one of your accounts is hacked.

The following is a *sample of a strong password technique.*

A strong password will be:

- At least eight characters long
- Different from other passwords
- Containing at least one character from each of the following categories:

    - Uppercase letters: A, B, C
    - Lowercase letters: a, b, c
    - Numbers: 0, 1, 2, 3, 4, 5, 6, 7, 8, 9
    - Symbols found on the keyboard: - + = { } [ ]
      \ ; " ' < > , . ? | ` ~ ! @ / # $ % ^ & * ( )/ _ :

A weak password includes:

- Your name, user name, or company name
- Less than 6 characters long
- Includes a complete word (example, Television)

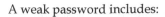

Changing passwords

The third step you can take to protect your accounts against unwanted attention is by changing your passwords on a routine basis. Consider the password attackers previously mentioned; these programs would theoretically be able to crack any password given enough time. Additionally, you should not consider your password completely secure even if a service, such as passfault, estimates the time to crack your password at over one century. New and more complex password attackers are being developed all the time, which can therefore significantly reduce the time to crack your passwords. Therefore, the easiest way you can reduce the likelihood that one of these programs might be able to hack your account information is by changing your passwords on a consistent schedule. Generally, you want to change your passwords at least once every three months. In addition to reducing the effectiveness of password attackers, changing your passwords can also combat the effectiveness of large-scale hacker attacks, such as the one mentioned against Twitter. After all, the login information obtained in such a hack is only effective if the information remains unchanged.

Data encryption

By encrypting your data, you can increase the difficulty entailed in hacking your device or personal accounts. Data encryption is a method of protection in which data is altered, or encrypted, using a **key**. With data encryption, the only parties able to access encrypted data are those that possess the key.

Some terms that you may encounter while learning how to encrypt your device are **data-in-transit**, **data-at-rest**, and **data-in-use**. All of these terms deal with how data is transferred and accessed in the context of data encryption. Data-in-transit and data-in-use are interchangeable terms, which refer to any data being accessed over a network. Examples of this type of data might be e-mails, websites, downloads, or uploads. Alternately, data-at-rest is any data not currently being accessed over a network. Examples of this type of data would include music residing on a portable hard drive or word processor documents, which are not currently being altered or e-mailed. When used, these terms often refer to how data encryption operates depending upon how it is being used or accessed.

Encryption on iOS

In the mobile space, data encryption is becoming increasingly common. As of release 5, iOS has encryption built into its operating system. IIRC, the key derived partly from the passcode and used for data protections, is used to encrypt certain data at rest on the device. By default, this is the e-mail store (messages and attachments), the keychain, and any third-party apps that have been written to make use of the data protection API.

To verify that this feature is active on your iPhone, iPad, or iPod, simply open the **Passcode Lock** submenu under **General Settings**, scroll to the bottom and look for the **Password Protection** subheader.

While the built-in data encryption is helpful, the feature does not extend to phone calls; if you wish to encrypt your outgoing phone calls, you will need to download some additional software. **Kryptos** and **Cellcrypt** are two of the better reviewed and regarded voice encryption apps currently available on the Apple App Store. To use this or any other encryption software, both the sender and the recipient must have the same encryption applications installed on both of their devices. Once installed, a user can simply place a call through the application, and the recipient will receive a notification on their device of the incoming phone call.

Encryption on Android

Android has had built-in full device encryption since Version 2.3.4 (Gingerbread) and all later versions of the OS (3.x, 4.x). They are some potential drawbacks, these being:

- Slower performance: Encryption always adds some overhead, so your device will be a bit slower. The actual performance decrease depends on the device hardware, and with modern multicore GHz clock speed CPUs is likely to be negligible.

- Encryption is one-way only: After encrypting your device's storage, you can only disable encryption by resetting your phone to its factory default settings (so make regular backups).

  It can be enabled via **Settings** | **Security** | **Encrypt phone** (or **Encrypt tablet**) under the **Encryption** subheading.

Downloaded applications

As of June of 2012, the Apple App Store contained over 650,000 apps, and over 30 billion app downloads had occurred since the store's launch (`http://mashable.com/2012/06/11/wwdc-2012-app-store-stats/`). By September of the same year, the Google Android Store achieved 25 billion downloads and hosted over 675,000 apps (`http://appleinsider.com/articles/12/09/26/google-android-reaches-25-billion-downloads-675000-apps`).

Considering the vast number of apps and large number of downloads, it should come as no surprise that Apple's and Google's attempts at policing their stores are not always successful. Admittedly, Google's Android Store contains more suspect apps than Apple's App Store; the first recorded instance of malicious software in Apple's App Store occurred in May 2012 (`http://www.wired.com/gadgetlab/2012/07/first-ios-malware-found/`). Regardless of which store they use, users should be vigilant in protecting themselves against this potential security risk. Users can follow two basic steps to protect themselves against malicious apps: install antivirus software on smartphone devices and take the time to research apps before downloading.

Antivirus software on smartphones

Antivirus software for smartphones is still relatively new as a category of program in the mobile space. This may be the reason that such a large number of smartphones still possess no installed antivirus software.

Obtaining antivirus software for your smartphone is a simple task. You should *not* conduct a search for "antivirus software" or a related term on your app store; you have no way of knowing that the apps returned in such a search are not themselves some form of malware. Instead, users should take care to download antivirus software from a respected and well-known developer. Norton and McAfee, for example, have both released smartphone antivirus suites, which you can download and install on your device for a fee. To find these apps on your preferred store, enter in the exact name of the antivirus suite you wish to download.

Verifying that an application is legitimate

The second step any user should follow to protect themselves against malicious or misleading apps is to take the time to research apps before choosing to download. Just because a user has installed antivirus software on the phone, they should not expect that this software will catch all possible threats; just as on personal computers, it is important to remember that new Trojans and viruses are being developed at an extremely rapid pace.

It can be tempting to rely on an app store's search feature; searching for a particular term and reading reviews in the store before downloading can seem a convenient method for obtaining new apps. You may even decide to simply download the top-rated result of a particular search. Unfortunately, the ratings and listing results on app store search engines are not a reliable measure of an application's quality or legitimacy.

For example, the Geinimi Trojan gains access to smartphones when users download a game entitled **Monkey Jump 2**. You may believe that any application with malware would likely have negative reviews; after all, why would a victim of a malware attack positively review a malicious application? Surprisingly, however, Monkey Jump 2 has relatively positive reviews on the Android store; it possesses over one-hundred and eighty 5-star reviews! Despite this rating, Monkey Jump 2 is one of over 30 apps on the Android store known to contain the Geinimi Trojan. If you were looking for a fun game and made the mistake of downloading this app based on positive reviews on the Android store, you might have unknowingly downloaded this devastating Trojan.

The easiest way to avoid downloading a malicious app is by taking the time to conduct some basic research through a traditional browser before downloading an app. If, for example, you wish to download a personal exercise trainer, you can simply enter some relevant search terms in your favorite search engine; **Top Exercise Trainers for iPhone** might be a good term. For additional security and reliability, you should consider only those results produced by a respected consumer or technology publication such as CNET or Wired; such publications routinely review certain categories of apps on both Apple and Android application stores.

Once you've chosen which application you wish to download based on reliable reviews, you should carefully enter the exact name of the application in your application store's search box. Do not omit any terms in the application's title. For example, if the name of the application is **Norton Security and Antivirus**, you should not type **Antivirus** into your application store's search box. While you are likely to obtain some of the same results, it is also possible that some illegitimate results may also appear. To avoid the risk of downloading one of these illegitimate or intentionally misleading applications, you should enter in the exact name of the application you wish to download.

In the event that your device has been compromised

Despite your best efforts, it is possible that your device or data may at some point suffer an attack. This can occur in multiple ways; the device may have been mistakenly left at a public place, or a hacker may have been successful in obtaining login information through a large-scale attack. Regardless of the reason, there are certain steps which you can take to mitigate the damages in the event that your device has been compromised.

Has your device been hacked?

First, you will need to verify that your devices or accounts have been hacked. Hackers will commonly use hacked devices to remotely send e-mails, place phone calls, or use SMS messaging. Therefore, users should carefully monitor their outgoing and incoming data. Also, watch out for when your device connects to a Wi-Fi hotspot, as some hotspots are hosted by hackers.

Have you received any strange texts from unknown senders? One method by which hackers attempt to hack smartphones is by sending SMS messages with embedded malware; all the recipient needs to do is open the text to download the malware. Texts with embedded malware often contain a square or other abstract symbol in the body of the text. If you have received this sort of a text, you may have unknowingly downloaded malware into your smartphone.

Users should carefully monitor their outgoing texts, phone calls, and e-mails. If a hacker has been using your device to send messages or place phone calls, it is likely that your call or message history will reflect this activity. Pay careful attention to any messages or calls that were placed at strange times, such as when you know you were sleeping or otherwise not likely to have been using your device. You should also check the content of suspect outgoing SMS messages or e-mails to verify that you typed and sent the particular message. If you think that your phone is sending out SMS messages due to malware, contact your provider as soon as possible.

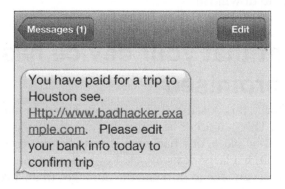

Often, hackers will use a compromised device to send messages to everyone in a user's contact list. If you discover that your device has been used for this purpose, you should immediately contact the individuals that received these messages and advise them not to open any links or attachments contained in such messages. By opening such links or attachments, the recipients could compromise their own devices or data. The previous example shows where a hacker is trying to get you to open a link via an SMS message.

Similarly, users should pay careful attention to activity in numerous online accounts. Facebook, Twitter, Paypal, personal banking, Amazon, eBay; these are only a few of the services that many users access through their smartphones. In the event that one of these accounts is hacked, it will be important to recognize the breach as quickly as possible so as to minimize the risk. Therefore, just as you should monitor your outgoing e-mails and SMS messages, you should also pay careful attention to your activities on these sorts of online accounts. As one example, if your Facebook friends suddenly begin to receive spam advertisements from your Facebook account, you should consider the possibility that your Facebook login has been hacked.

Social engineering

Social engineering is the process of manipulating people into sharing their personal information. This can be executed in several ways; one way is to talk a person into answering questions from a supposed authority. For example, you think that your company calls you and says, "We are from your corporate help desk, we need to confirm your password." In this example the "hacker" is not from your company and is trying to extract your password from you. There are many different types of social engineering and these are discussed in the previous chapters. Overall the rule is *never* to give out information to people that call you; but there can be cases where you think you called the right place. In all cases, be careful and make sure you know who you are talking with before you share any information over the phone!

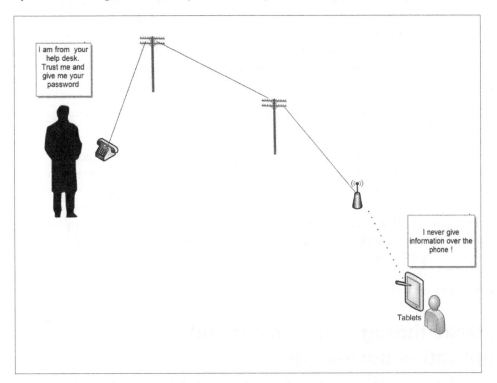

Trojans and malware on your smartphone

Your device may download a Trojan or malware through various methods: an SMS text message, a compromised Wi-Fi hotspot, a downloaded application, or an e-mail attachment. Depending upon the exact avenue of access, as well as the particular Trojan or malware, the best course of action can vary significantly.

SMS messaging attacks

Those Trojans that access a smartphone through a suspect SMS message are among the most damaging to a device; the surest sign that you were the recipient of such a message is if the body of the message contains nothing more than an abstract symbol, such as a circle or square. Commonly, this type of Trojan will automatically install the moment the user opens the text; this Trojan will thereafter allow a hacker to remotely access and control the device.

Unfortunately, the possible responses to this particular type of attack are relatively limited. Significantly, smartphone antivirus programs have been largely unsuccessful at isolating this threat. According to security researcher Charles Miller, the best course of action is to immediately power off the device; the longer the device is left on with the offending Trojan installed, the greater the possible damage to the user's personal identity. After all, if the hacker can remotely control the device, they then have a method of accessing a user's personal accounts through any downloaded applications or even through the user's browser history. Though an old attack, it is worth noting:

```
http://www.ibtimes.com/what-do-if-your-iphone-gets-hacked-
virus-302908
```

The user should then bring the device to a service provider or manufacturer storefront at the earliest possible convenience. The device should remain powered off in the interim, as turning on the device will only allow the Trojan to reactivate. As an example, if the device is an iPhone, the user should bring the device to the nearest Apple location. Alternately, if the device is an Android phone, the best option will likely be the nearest service provider's storefront. Often, these storefront locations will opt to wipe the device and restore it to factory settings, in the process removing all offending data. Users should follow up this activity by taking the steps listed in the section on compromised accounts.

Attacks through attachment and application downloads

The other two methods, by which a hacker may access a device, downloading applications or downloading attachments, are rarely as devastating as the SMS text method. This is because, unlike with the SMS text method, the user may avoid downloading the Trojan or malware in the first place. By conducting some research about an application and by deciding not to download any attachments from untrusted sources, users can reduce the likelihood that they will allow a hacker access to their device.

In the event that a user believes they downloaded a Trojan or malware, they should first run a virus scan through their smartphone's antivirus software. Often, the software will be able to apprehend offending downloads even before a user decides to run a scan. Even so, users should remain vigilant and run scans on a scheduled basis so as to catch any additional threats. In the event that the antivirus successfully recognizes and isolates an offending virus, the user should consider that the virus may have been successful at hacking any accounts accessed by the device. As in the event of an SMS message attack, users should follow the advice contained in the following section on compromised accounts. Users should also carefully monitor their outgoing SMS text messages and phone calls; if you noticed any suspect messages or calls, you should immediately bring the device into the nearest manufacturer or cell-carrier storefront for a factory reset and data wipe.

Compromised accounts

Compromised login information is one of the most significant threats in mobile security. A device may be repaired or replaced, but a hacked account can significantly impact your identity and personal finances. If you believe that login information for one of your accounts may have been compromised, there are steps that you may take to limit the damage.

Check out `http://www.sophos.com/en-us/medialibrary/PDFs/other/sophossecuritythreatreport2013.pdf`.

Regardless of the type of account that was compromised, the first step a user should take is try to access their account from a different device. This will allow you to see if you can get into your account and/or change your password. Do not continue to use your smartphone to manage the account in question; instead use a laptop or personal computer until the threat has been sufficiently managed. From a computer, the user should log in to the account and change the login password. Most accounts will have a link within the personal settings of an account where this may be easily and quickly done.

Depending upon the type of account and upon the activities for which the account was used, the user may wish to change the login ID as well as the password. For most accounts, such as Facebook or Twitter, this cannot be done without contacting customer service by phone or e-mail. If a service is unable or unwilling to allow this change, you may wish to consider deleting the old account entirely and creating a new one. If you think you have an issue with an e-mail account, check the forwarding settings to see if the mail is being redirected.

If the account was used for financial transactions or banking account management, the repercussions may be more severe. For example, if a user's Amazon shopping account information was compromised, they should follow the steps of checking your password and login ID. In addition to these changes, however, the user should also contact their banks for any associated credit cards. Your bank should be notified as early as possible if such an account is expected to be compromised.

The user should also monitor and, if necessary, dispute any questionable charges with their bank. Similar steps should be taken if the account in question was an online banking profile; most banks possess advanced responses to these increasingly common situations.

Many sites will have a set of URLs/pages that provide information if your account is compromised, for example:

*   `http://windows.microsoft.com/en-GB/windows/outlook/hacked-account`

*   `https://www.facebook.com/hacked`

Stolen or lost devices

In the event that your device has been lost or stolen, you can potentially wipe the device's data remotely to protect against the possibility that any account used on the device will be compromised. Increasingly, companies have begun to rely on this method to mitigate these sorts of risks. As part of these capabilities, companies may decide to either partially or completely wipe a device. In a partial wipe, only certain data considered sensitive will be deleted from the device. Alternately, in a complete wipe, all data and the device's operating system will be altered so as to make the device practically unusable via a remote lock. Today, you as a user may be able to conduct a complete wipe depending upon your particular device and MDM solution.

Wiping an iOS device

In the event that your iOS device has been lost or stolen, you can decide to remotely wipe it. However, you may wish to first utilize the iCloud's **Find my iPhone** feature to verify that the device was not lost in a safe place such as your home or vehicle. The **Find my iPhone** feature is available as an application download for your iOS device, or by logging into `icloud.com` and clicking on the related **Find my iPhone** link. This feature utilizes the iCloud to locate the GPS signal of your device provided the device is powered on. Remember that you must first turn on the **Find my iPhone** feature on your device while it is still in your possession; you can do this by accessing the iCloud submenu within the **Settings** tab on your iOS device.

Should you decide that you wish to completely wipe your device after conducting this search, you can do so either by using the Find my iPhone app or by logging into `icloud.com`. In either case, your iOS device's data will be wiped; it will have effectively been reset to its factory default configuration.

Wiping an Android device

One option that you can use to lock your Android is the **Android Lost** app to perform some of the same features as Apple's Find my iPhone application. Check out `https://play.google.com/store/apps/details?id=com.androidlost&hl=en`. With Android Lost, a user can read the device's SMS text messages, set an alarm on the device, locate the device through its GPS signal, or wipe the device's data. Like with iOS devices, this wipe feature will effectively reset the device to its factory default configuration. In other words, this will not be a complete wipe rendering the device unusable; it will merely prevent another person from accessing any data or applications you added to the device after purchase.

Summing up

Smartphone capabilities will undoubtedly continue to expand just as they have over the past decade. More and more users rely on these multifunctional devices to conduct sensitive tasks such as personal banking and shopping. Therefore, it should come as no surprise that hackers consider smartphones an enticing, and an all-too-often accessible target.

By taking a number of preventative steps, you can increase the difficulty entailed in hacking your device and personal accounts. While such steps will not create an iron-clad barrier to attacks, they can decrease the likelihood of a successful attack on your smartphone. The best way to consider such steps may be by comparing smartphone security to home security; bars and alarm systems will not make home intrusions impossible, but they will present enough difficulty to persuade many would-be criminals to search for easier targets. The same concept applies to preventative steps such as creating strong passwords, changing your passwords often, encrypting your data, and installing antivirus software on your smartphone. Faced with such measures, many hackers will search for easier targets.

In the case that your device is hacked, there are essentially four steps that you can take:

- Run the antivirus software
- Return your device to a storefront for a factory reset
- Change passwords and user IDs
- Monitor your device and accounts to ensure that the issue has been resolved

Depending on the issue, it may not always be necessary to return your device to a storefront for a factory reset. However, you should always run an antivirus software and change your user IDs and passwords after any incident. Finally, if your device should be stolen or lost, you should remotely wipe the data from the phone to protect your personal information. The next chapter will walk you through warranty and insurance for your device.

Summary

In this chapter, we discussed:

- Personal and device identification numbers
- Preventative measures to discourage hackers
- How to create strong passwords
- The disadvantages of reusing passwords
- Data encryption on smartphones
- How to research apps
- Signs that a device has been hacked
- SMS messaging attacks
- Trojans in applications and attachments
- What to do if an account has been compromised
- How to wipe a smartphone

In the next chapter we will see how to get your device serviced in the event of a significant malfunction.

6
Support and Warranty Insurance

In this chapter, we will help the user navigate the often complicated world of modern customer service and technical support. Also, this chapter will detail the concepts of support, warranty, and insurance for your mobile device. Included in this chapter are the following topics:

- Toby's story – this could be your story
- Determine the ownership of your phone and the impact on you
- The world of mobile support
- Your company's support processes and rules
- Why you should care about your company's Service Level Agreements (SLAs)
- How you can tell if you have a problem with your device
- Warranties – what you should know

Toby's story

Toby travels weekly for work. He flies to distant locations, conducts his business, and often returns home for the weekend. Occasionally, he might even be required to stay for extended time periods without returning home. To conduct company business, Toby relies on a number of vital devices: his laptop, a company-based server, his smartphone, and his personal tablet. Each device is useful for completing specific tasks. On his laptop, for example, he completes the most complex tasks, such as creating or modifying company documents. Toby uses his home-based server to run power-hungry applications, which his laptop is incapable of running. Toby's tablet is useful as a way of bringing up documents for easy perusal and sharing; Toby might, for instance, bring up an attachment from an e-mail and hand the tablet to a colleague for consideration.

Toby's smartphone may be his most important device. In the modern mobile world, Toby uses his smartphone for e-mail, texting, chatting, updating his personal calendar, organizing contacts, and even tasks that he normally completes on his laptop, such as modifying and creating documents. While Toby's laptop is his company's approved device, and is thus the only device his company explicitly supports for completing company tasks, Toby nevertheless opts to use his smartphone for many of these tasks. Toby's smartphone is a personal device, which he has decided to use at his place of work; it is therefore an expression of **Bring Your Own Device (BYOD)** practices, wherein personal devices are used for professional purposes.

One week while on business to Toledo, Toby decided to leave his laptop at home because he knew he could complete the necessary tasks for his assignment from his smartphone. On the first day of his assignment, Toby accidentally dropped his smartphone down the stairs. Picking it up, he discovered that the device would not start up. To continue doing business, Toby absolutely had to resolve this issue in a quick and efficient manner, because he did not have his laptop to complete basic tasks such as accessing company e-mail. Toby decided to call his company's technical support line. After all, Toby reasoned, the company technical support department had previously assisted in replacing and repairing his company laptop not two years prior. He assumed that they would easily be able to solve this problem as well.

Unfortunately for Toby, the technical support department's response was that Toby must contact his phone carrier's technical support department. Their reason? Toby's smartphone was not provided by the company, but was rather Toby's personal device, which he had purchased from his carrier as part of his cell-phone plan. Therefore, even though Toby *was* required to use the device for vital company tasks, the device's maintenance was Toby's responsibility alone. As noted, Toby is "required" to use the smartphone for vital company tasks and processes. This is an important point and one that sits at the heart of the BYOD debate. Continuing this story, we find that Toby decided to call his carrier's technical support. After waiting on the line for half an hour, Toby was greeted by a technical support representative over the phone. Toby informed the representative that his smartphone was broken, and asked if his carrier could provide him with a repair or replacement. Once again, the response was not what Toby wanted to hear; the representative told him that he would need to call the manufacturer's technical support line, and that his carrier's technical support would not be able to assist him with hardware malfunctions.

Becoming increasingly frustrated, Toby dialed the manufacturer's technical support number as the proper party to assist him with hardware malfunctions. After waiting for over an hour, Toby was finally able to speak to a technical support representative that would be able to assist him. The response was, once again, not encouraging. While the manufacturer would be able to provide Toby with a replacement device, Toby would have to spend a considerable amount of money to obtain it. This was because, the manufacturer's representative informed him, Toby's device was no longer under warranty. Additionally, the representative informed Toby that, even if the device had been within the warranty period, the manufacturer may not have been able to replace it because Toby's mistake in dropping the phone did not count as "normal use." Incensed, Toby pulled out his credit card and prepared to pay for his clumsiness.

The smartphone – a personal device, a company device, or both?

Toby's story is becoming increasingly common in the mobile world. Not so many years ago, most devices vital for conducting company business were mostly provided by the company. Therefore, when issues with the devices arose, employees could simply contact the company's technical support departments to have any issues resolved. This is still the case when the device is company-owned; many laptops, for instance, are still provided by companies and are therefore company-owned. Alternately, smartphones can be employee-owned. The company does not provide these devices to the employee and does not provide funding for the purchase of these devices; the employee is expected to purchase these devices and use them to complete company tasks.

As discussed previously, this is commonly referred to as BYOD. In most cases, when a BYOD smartphone malfunctions or breaks, the employee is expected to resolve the issue on their own. Consequently, if the employee is unable to complete company tasks due to a malfunctioning or broken smartphone, the employee may not blame this lack of productivity on their broken device. Many companies will publish a policy that the employee is responsible for the maintenance of their BYOD device. Customer service is something that is overlooked by most people, until they need it. We want to help you be prepared before you need help. Resolving issues with a malfunctioning or broken smartphone thus results in the same sorts of issues common to repairing or replacing any personal devices. For example, if your television breaks, you do not expect your employer to replace or repair it. This is because you purchased it with your own funds and you rarely, if ever, use it to complete company tasks. The same reasoning applies to your smartphone, except that you do use the device to complete company as well as personal tasks. In other words, because the phone was purchased with personal funds, it normally will be addressed the same as any other personally-purchased device that malfunctions or breaks. In the case of a device/phone provided by the employee, there may be policy issues where the company will not allow you to use the phone for personal use, and the inverse can be true where if the device breaks, then the company will replace it free of charge. As we have noted several times, make sure you know what your company policy states.

The wide world of customer service and technical support

To resolve customer issues, companies have developed customer support systems that can address seemingly any issue a customer might have. These processes are accessed by customers through a variety of means; chat, SMS, phone, and even in person at brick-and-mortar stores. Of all of these methods, the phone-operated system may be the most familiar to many customers.

- Dial 1. Want to claim a rebate?
- Dial 2. Is your hardware malfunctioning?
- Dial 3. Have billing questions?
- Dial 4. Are you having a software issues?

By using such a system, companies can funnel particular issues to relevant personnel that can best help resolve a customer's issue.

Decades ago, it was common for customers to bring their devices to an independent repair outlet at a strip mall. Today, however, it is far more common for a customer to contact a manufacturer to have a product repaired or replaced. The reasons for the decline of third-party repair solutions are numerous: the use of proprietary parts by manufacturers, the fact that replacement is often cheaper than repair and, in smartphones, the entangled relationship between our cell-phone plan and our devices.

What happens if you cannot get help from your vendor and/or the vendor does not provide help in the way you need or expect? You escalate the call. Many vendors will give you a call tracking number. If you are not happy with the services, ask the vendor to escalate the call. The following is a sample flow chart on how you can do this:

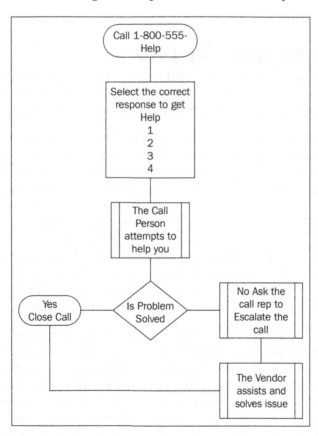

Customer support in the mobile space – phone, chat, and text

As previously discussed, customer support systems can be accessed through numerous methods. Seemingly any method by which you might contact an individual can also be used to contact a company's customer support. Believe it or not, some companies still allow customers to send their customer support departments inquiries by postal mail. Of course, that method is becoming less and less common, as contacting such departments by other methods is far more efficient and helps resolve issues in a timely manner. Online call requests allow for better tracking of service calls.

Customer support by phone

This is the most common, and some might argue, a highly developed method by which customer service issues are resolved. Customer support systems can be divided into three basic categories of operations: **personal**, **automated**, and **hybrid**.

A personal customer support system would be a phone system where, upon dialing a company's customer support phone number, a customer would be greeted immediately by an in-person representative. Exclusively personal customer support systems are becoming increasingly rare; a customer is most likely to encounter these sorts of low-tech systems at independent or small companies, where customer volume is relatively low. The advantage of these systems is that a customer will be able to speak with a representative immediately and will in this manner be able to bypass the automated protocols present in automated and hybrid customer service systems. The disadvantage of this system is that, in able to reach the correct department within a business, a caller may have to explain their problem numerous times to different individuals. In other words, the system can be inefficient in certain circumstances.

An automated customer support system is one in which all customer support is conducted exclusively through an automated phone system. In this system, an automated voice message plays that informs a caller of which selections to make from a list of pre-designated choices. The two primary methods by which customers may navigate these automated systems is touchtone and voice-operated. For the former, callers will press the corresponding number on their phones to select a choice. For the latter, callers will speak a particular keyword, often in the form of a number, to make their selections.

The exclusively automated system is advantageous when it comes to delivering limited information or to addressing common complaints. For example, a company might be aware that a large number of callers only call to request the address or business hours of a company, so the company may set up a separate line to provide just this information. These automated systems can also handle higher levels of call traffic. The caller will be able to access the desired information in a quick manner, and the company would not have to sacrifice productivity in man-hours to provide this information to customers. The disadvantages of this system become apparent when customers wish to obtain solutions to more complicated problems. For example, if a customer is having difficulty operating their smartphone because they downloaded an application that causes bugs on a percentage of devices, an automated system may not be the most ideal method for resolving this issue. This is because automated systems are, by their nature, best suited for addressing issues and questions that are common to most or all customers. A problem that manifests in only some users requires more layers of complexity within an automated system, thus defeating an automated system's original advantage; efficiency.

The hybrid system is a system that utilizes both automation and personal support methods. This system has become the most common customer support system utilized by large companies, such as cell phone carriers and smartphone manufacturers. In a hybrid system, callers will often initially be forced to navigate an automated message system. They will dial or say their choices and only be able to speak in person with a representative after they have exhausted the choices contained within the automated system. Often, this corresponds to a certain number of "layers" of messages within the automated system. At this point, the caller will often be provided with an option with the following or similar wording; "Speak with a customer service representative if your issue has still not been resolved." After choosing to speak to a representative, the caller will be placed in a queue and wait until a representative is available to speak with them.

Often, hybrid systems will be integrated on a department-by-department basis. What this means for the caller is that, should they progress through the automated system to a representative in one department, and should that representative need to transfer them to another department, the caller would then need to progress through the automated system of the other department as well. This system is advantageous for the company because it helps reduce the number of calls that representatives must spend their man-hours addressing; each department will be able to provide solutions to the most common problems in their automated systems. The disadvantage of this system is that, for those customers who need to address less common problems, customers will be forced to spend extra time navigating not one but two or even more automated systems before being funneled to the correct personnel; also in some cases customers can be stuck in an endless loop without getting their problem fixed.

Although many express frustration at having to deal with automated customer support systems, it is important to remember that these systems, when implemented properly, can greatly increase the efficiency of company personnel in addressing the more complicated and uncommon customer issues. Imagine, for example, if every customer with a complex issue had to wait for every customer with a question about their current account balance before they could be helped. Of course, some companies have attempted to address customer antipathy toward automated systems by hiring more personnel to replace their automated systems, but these solutions are often prohibitively costly for smaller or medium-sized companies. As a result, we can probably expect that automated voice systems will be a prominent, and even growing, part of our interactions with customer support systems for the foreseeable future.

Chat and texting solutions

As the Internet becomes an increasingly pervasive aspect of our lives, companies are beginning to provide methods by which customers can contact their support systems online. One reason that customer and technical support systems have not been provided online is that, until recently, many customers only had a limited number of methods by which to access the Internet. Meaning, if a customer's laptop was broken, and this was their only Internet-connected device, providing a chat option for customer service would be not be a cost-effective decision. Today, however, many customers have a laptop, a tablet, a smartphone, and a desktop that can all connect to the Internet simultaneously. In such a context, it makes sense for companies to provide an online method for contacting their customer support, as it will have the benefit of removing some of the burden placed on their phone support system.

The methods by which online support can be accessed are often restricted to a form of Internet chatting, whereby a customer will type their question in on an Internet-connected device, and a representative will answer their question in a text response. Some companies, however, are beginning to offer voice and video chatting solutions as part of their online customer support solutions, but these are still fairly uncommon as of the time of writing. Companies also provide intelligent response systems, where questions and answers can be provided based on specific issues, for example: "Have you tried..." Then, if this automated system is not able to fix the issue, you will be transferred to a representative. As an example, Verizon wireless provides customers with the ability to connect to a customer or technical support representative immediately through a chat application implemented on the company's website. Additionally, the correct department can be immediately accessed by simply clicking on the department's chat link. Unlike with the automated phone system, a customer does not need to navigate a general automated system before being funneled to the correct department.

Additionally, should a customer need to speak with a different representative, within many chat services, a user can be automatically and instantaneously transferred to a representative in the correct department. Often, this results in a far more efficient and speedy customer service system compared with the more common phone-operated customer service systems.

Some customer support systems implement a hybrid of phone-operated and Internet-based customer methods. Often, this takes the form of a request by the automated phone system to the user that they fill out an online form with relevant information about their issue. Then, they are requested to redial the customer support number. Alternately, some businesses allow a user to fill out a request online, and then they are contacted by a customer service representative by phone and the issue is resolved based on the information the user submitted online.

SMS text

SMS text messaging is becoming increasingly common as a supplementary method of delivering customer service. In practice, this customer service solution works the same as a text chatting customer service system; a user will send a text message to a designated customer service number, and then will be given responses via a text message from that number. As with text messaging, this is advantageous because it allows a user to bypass the often frustrating automated voice systems present in phone-operated customer service systems. In the future, it is likely that businesses will develop new methods for providing customer support in the mobile space. Right now, the primary method is through text message, but we would not be surprised if, in the near future, businesses began to provide voice and video customer service through a mobile phone application similar to Skype.

One cool feature today is the ability for a company to take remote control of your system. This is not automatic and by default companies will not attempt this. Also, in many cases special software needs to be installed and/or executed. This is a risk—make sure you know the company and that you called the company and the company did *not* call you. Once the company is connected to your device, they can diagnose the issues and install fixes and/or send you a fix as needed.

This is an age old issue. Never give out information and/or allow access to your personal positions if someone has *called* you. There are always risks with giving access to your devices for remote control. The risk is very high if someone calls you and says, "I am from your help desk, I need remote access to your device." Make sure you know who *you are* calling and if in doubt, don't allow access or disconnect the network connection. Please don't get us wrong on this point, you can be ask risk *even if you make a call*. If you think that someone has connected to your system without authority, then call your company security department and your service provider and ask for help. If in doubt, *don't* allow access.

The Service Level Agreement (SLA)

It is important for you, the end user, to understand the various types of Service Level Agreements that can impact you. Understanding SLAs can provide information on what you can expect from your company and/or your service provider. For example, will your company help you 24 hours a day for 7 days a week, or just Monday to Friday? For companies, providing customer service and technical support for their products can be a costly and daunting endeavor. Primarily, this is due to the vast breadth of services, which must be provided for any released product. Consider a cell phone plan. A carrier must not only provide cell phone service to its customers; it must also develop a system for addressing customer concerns and to ensure that their cell phone service is meeting or exceeding customer expectations. Otherwise, of course, the carrier risks losing its customers to rivals. To meet customer expectations, a company must provide a customer-friendly method for addressing concerns.

These include the following:

- Account services, such as balances or adjusting payment methods
- Problems with service, such as outages or dropped calls
- Sales issues, such as hardware or plan upgrades
- Technical services, such as setup assistance or technical support

All these services address numerous problems, which fall into each corresponding category. To address this vast array of issues, companies have developed guidelines that specify the exact scope of service, which they will be willing to provide to their customers for any released product. These guidelines are called **Service Level Agreements (SLAs)**.

SLAs may be considered as a form of liability protection from the perspective of a company, as they specify both the extent and limits of service, which customers might expect. For example, an SLA agreement might contain information regarding those cases in which hardware malfunctions will be covered under the company's manufacturer warranty. This detail would, by extension, also reveal those situations in which the manufacturer would *not* replace or repair hardware without charging the customer.

Similarly, an SLA might also provide specifics on the amount of time a customer might wait before their call is addressed, or on the priority particular customer issues might be given within the company's support structure. High priority issues might be a cell phone, which is unable to make or receive calls. An example of a lower priority issue may be password recovery in the case of a customer that forgot their account password.

SLAs are important to you, the end user, because they clearly define the extent of services that you can expect and even demand if you feel that your needs are not being met. Alternately, of course, SLAs can also indicate the limits of a company's services. In most cases, SLAs can be easily located on a company's website. One example is `https://business.verizon.com/MyBusinessAccount/one.portal?_nfpb=true&_pageLabel=gb_policy&page_id=tos_fios_biz_bef_jan92006`. Within the context of customer service and technical support, SLAs clearly define a number of expected metrics. These can range from the time it takes in seconds for a call to be answered to the percentage of calls in which the user disconnected while waiting for a representative. While, internally, SLAs are an important method for assessing efficiency within a technical support system, for the end user, these same SLAs can be used as a method of determining what sort of service you can expect when you call.

The following points show where you can start to get to know your SLAs:

- Ask your company what service levels they offer/support
- Ask your service provider what service level they offer
- Also, check with your hardware vendor (or extended warranty) what service levels they offer

OS operators, manufacturers, and service providers

Depending on a smartphone's error, it is not always easy to know which company to call. For example, imagine that your iPhone spontaneously powers off every time you attempt to load your Angry Birds game application. In this case, you have three possible customer or technical support parties that you could contact: the Angry Birds developer Rovio, Apple's technical support for assistance with its hardware or OS, or your cell phone carrier (AT&T, Verizon Wireless, and so on). In this case, it is unlikely to be an issue with your cell phone carrier; the problem is more likely associated with the iPhone software or hardware, or with the Angry Birds application itself. As you can see, though, deciding which party to contact for technical support can sometimes be a difficult decision when it comes to your smartphone. Although one could decide to call each number until they get the solution they want, most of us would prefer to spend as little time as possible on the phone talking to technical support representatives.

The following three categories are the most common categories for technical support parties. However, it is important to keep in mind that these categories are not iron-clad, as they do overlap in some cases. The previous example of the iPhone is one such case; Apple is the party to contact regarding both hardware and software issues. This is because, unlike other companies, Apple both develops the software and produces the hardware for its products. This may be contrasted with numerous Windows and Android phones, wherein the manufacturer and the software developers are different companies.

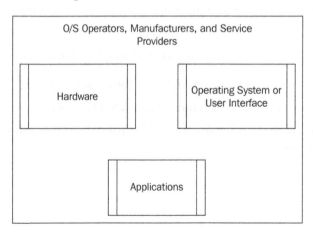

Hardware

You should contact the manufacturer of your device if you have a hardware malfunction. Toby's example from the beginning of this chapter is a good example of a hardware malfunction; he dropped his phone and now the device will not work. Other examples of hardware malfunctions would be broken or cracked cases, water damage, and sun damage. In addition to these easily observable malfunctions, however, there are also numerous other nonvisible malfunctions, which are issues with the hardware rather than the software or applications.

Other device issues

Imagine that you turned on your smartphone one day and discovered that it failed to load your normal home screen. In other words, your smartphone was unable to launch its operating system. In this case, your smartphone may have experienced a hardware failure in the form of memory corruption. This could also be a processor malfunction or failure as well. These sorts of errors do not always occur from dropping or otherwise, physically damaging a device; they can occur from normal usage, thus seeming spontaneous to the average user.

Generally, a user may assume that an error or malfunction is a hardware issue if their phone is exhibiting one of the following examples:

- Discolored screen
- Distorted or "fuzzy" reception on calls or in music playback
- Cracked, peeling, or otherwise damaged casing on the device
- Failure to boot to the home screen (inability to load the operating system)
- Embedded operating system issues
- Device spontaneously powers off without user input
- Inability to turn on device (can be a broke device and/or firmware)

Operating system or user interface

You should contact your operating system or user interface developer if your device is experiencing a software error related to the device's basic interface. Every smartphone utilizes an operating system. The three most common mobile operating systems are as follows:

- iOS
- Android
- Windows

In the case of iOS, Apple is both the developer and manufacturer. However, in the cases of Android and Windows phones, the user will need to determine if the error is hardware or software in nature, and then to contact the appropriate party. This is a key point—be sure and ask the sales person (or website)—who you should contact if you have an issue. The answer may not always be the company that makes the OS.

Here are a few examples of errors relating to the interface of an operating system for a smartphone. Imagine that you turned on your Windows phone, and it was able to load the home screen without issue. If you were then unable to load your phone's factory-installed e-mail application, and that attempting to load this application caused your phone to turn off altogether, this would likely be an error with the operating system or user interface. In this case, a user should contact the vendor technical support to resolve this issue, as it would most likely be an issue related to the operation of Windows on the smartphone. Another example of this sort of malfunction might be an inability to load a contact list, calendar, or to access the general settings on a device. Essentially, if a user is able to load the phone into the operating system, but is unable to access factory-installed or pre-installed applications or features, then the malfunction is likely to be an operating system or user interface error.

If a user experiences any of the following errors, he/she may assume that his/her phone is experiencing an operating system or user-interface error:

- Inability to load device settings
- Inability to load various factory-installed applications
- Phone crashes when attempting to access essential applications
- User is unable to change or update settings

Application issues

A user should contact the developer of a particular application if the error is isolated to the operation of the application and does not seem to be replicated with any other applications. Application errors are relatively common; how many times have you attempted to load an application after downloading it from the App store, only to discover that it fails to load or occasionally crashes while in use? Often, applications may experience difficulties if they were designed with an earlier operating system release in mind and were not updated to account for recent releases. In other cases, the applications themselves were simply not adequately bug tested before release, and thus some users experience problems with an application.

Determining whether the issue is an application malfunction or an operating system malfunction can be difficult due to the nature of modern smartphones. Often, what may appear to be an error related to a particular application may actually be a more generalized malfunction within the operating system or even, occasionally, the hardware itself. The main criteria that might reveal your error as an application error is that the malfunction or issue is isolated within one particular application. For example, if your Angry Birds game application continually crashes, but if no other applications are exhibiting a similar behavior, then your error may be an application malfunction. Similarly, if your Twitter application fails to load, but all other applications operate normally, and you are experiencing no other issues in any other aspect of your phone, the error is probably an application malfunction.

To verify that a malfunction is an application malfunction, a user should take the following steps:

1. Determine which particular actions are causing the error (for example; loading the application, adjusting settings within the application, or performing a particular task within the application). Your support team may ask you if you can run the application on a difference device.

2. Open another application, and perform a similar task. If the error does not occur within another application, continue testing; a user should test at least three applications before making a determination.

3. If the error occurs in the other application, the issue is *not* with the particular application, but is likely an operating system or hardware malfunction.

4. If the error *does not* occur with any other applications, then the error is likely an application error related to one particular application.

5. Before calling customer service or technical support, a user should uninstall the application and re-download it. Contact customer service only if the error continues to occur after re-installing and running the application.

How to get the most out of your technical support experience if you have a malfunction

Even after determining that you have a malfunction, there are still a number of steps that should be taken before picking up the phone. While it may be tempting to simply make the call and work out the details as you go, you may find that, by taking the time to prepare the necessary information and complete some essential research, you can greatly reduce the amount of time spent on the phone. Additionally, you will likely find that the quality of the assistance you're given is greater.

Before you make the call – information, password problems, and your malfunction

The first step to take before contacting customer service is to ensure that you have all the information, which they might request, already in front of you. This might include your address, credit card information, and account information. All information that you think might be relevant to your device should be prepared in advance; this includes basic personal information, which most customer service systems require to validate your identity. By preparing this information, you will be able to reduce the amount of time spent on preliminary questions before addressing the specifics of your malfunction. This information can also be useful before speaking to a representative, as it can assist you with navigating the automated touchtone menu that many customer service systems utilize.

You should also familiarize yourself with your device's warranty information. In some cases, your malfunction may render your device irreparable. For this reason, you should take the time to become familiar with warranty information, so that you understand whether the company will be able to replace your device. Information to which you should pay particular attention to is whether certain malfunctions will be considered as "normal use". The implications of this term will be discussed further on.

In addition to personal and device information, you should also be prepared to describe in detail the exact nature of your problem. This will enable support to find the issues quickly and/or see if support can repair the issues. For example, if the error seems to be an application error, you should be prepared to describe exactly how the error is manifested. Does it occur after loading an application, or only after performing a particular task? Does the application run effectively if you avoid performing a particular task, or does it crash after a certain amount of time without input? If you believe that describing the specifics of your malfunction will be challenging, do not hesitate to write or type some notes for your personal reference. By writing down the exact steps under which your malfunction occurs, you may find that describing it to a representative will be easier.

The following is a checklist of information, which you should prepare before contacting customer service or technical support:

- Account-holder's personal information (name, address, and other personal details)
- Account username and password

[Provided in *Chapter 8, Getting Your Life Back After You've Been Hacked,* is a tracking checklist for customer service and technical support.]

- Warranty information (or extended warranty)
- Device-specific information (the device's serial number or model ID)
- Desired department (billing, technical support, hardware department, software department) – this is very important with BYOD and/or company assigned devices
- If necessary, prepare a written or typed outline of the nature of your malfunction

How to make the most of your time while on the line

You've spent five minutes navigating the company's touchtone system, and another fifteen minutes waiting on hold for a representative. Now, it is important that you take steps to ensure that your problem is addressed adequately and thoroughly. Otherwise, you may find yourself starting the process all over again once you realize that the malfunction has not been fixed.

Three important steps can be taken to obtain the best results from customer service and technical support representatives:

[Please be polite and remain calm, remember the representative is only doing their job!]

- Answer every question the representative asks.
- Do not "skip" steps when describing your problem to a representative.
- Be sure and get the representative's name and the call number. This is an opportunity for you to log your steps and who you spoke with. This information may be important later.
- Test your device numerous times before concluding your call.

Answer every question

Customer service representatives are often trained based on a "script"; a set of questions that they are required to ask in a particular order. These scripts vary from company to company, but many utilize similar questions. For example, one common preliminary question for customer support scripts at computer companies is related to the power supply of a device; "is your device plugged in?"

Basic questions, such as these, can be frustrating to answer, as many callers will be knowledgeable enough to have checked into these matters themselves before calling customer service. However, it's important to remember that these questions *are* applicable to enough customers to justify their inclusion in the company's "script".

Imagine how much time might be wasted if a customer called in about a malfunctioning computer only to discover that, an hour later, they had forgotten to plug it into the outlet. By including these basic questions, customer service representatives can address those callers with the simplest issues in a short and effective manner.

Basically, take the time to help the representative; in this way they will able to more effectively pinpoint the nature of your malfunction.

Do not skip steps when describing your problem

If possible, you should refrain from the temptation to "skip" basic steps when describing the nature of your malfunction to a customer service representative. Basic steps might include: turning on the device, loading the offending application, or entering your password information. While it may seem intuitive to think that the representative will know that you have taken these steps to arrive at your malfunction, it is important to remember that the representative cannot see or interact with your device personally. The representative is entirely reliant on you to provide them with detailed information so that they can accurately conceptualize how the malfunction occurs on your device. If you leave out basic information, you may unknowingly provide the representative with an inaccurate understanding of your device's malfunction, which might then lead to an inaccurate diagnosis of the problem.

Test your device

At the end of your call, you have hopefully been able to resolve your malfunction, and your device is working properly once again. However, you should hold the representative on the line until after you have verified that the malfunction has actually been fixed. For example, if the malfunction occurs while loading your smartphone's e-mail application, you should load the application numerous times to test it. You may also wish to power off your device, then power it on and test the application once again. Only after numerous tests should you allow the representative to disconnect; after all, you don't want to have to start the customer support process over from the beginning.

What to do if your malfunction has not been resolved

If, at the conclusion of the call, your problem has *not* been resolved, do not allow the representative to refuse responsibility for the error. Assuming that you have performed the steps previously listed to verify the nature of your malfunction, you should be confident that you have contacted the proper party. Therefore, you should insist that the representative addresses your malfunction and assists you with a resolution. If necessary, be prepared to request to speak to another representative or to the representative's supervisor. Be firm; this is their product, after all.

In some cases, the malfunction may be serious enough to render your device irreparable. Assuming that you took the preliminary steps, you will be aware of your rights as they relate to the company's warranty policy. While a representative is unlikely to misrepresent their company's warranty policy, you should still consider it your own responsibility to ensure that a company follows their warranty policies to the letter.

Warranties in the mobile space

Warranties are not new, and have been provided for seemingly countless commodities for decades. Smartphones present new challenges to the old warranty models because these devices are often simultaneously covered by their manufacturer and the cellular provider. Navigating this web of warranties to determine which one applies can be challenging. With some basic information, a user can determine the extent and limitations of warranties on their smartphones.

Basic terms

Go into a big-box store and purchase an item. In all likelihood, you will be offered an extended warranty of one type or another. Depending on the item, the price and duration of this warranty may fluctuate greatly. For a new television, for example, the warranty might cost thirty-five dollars and cover your television for damages for a period of three years. You may even be offered the opportunity to extend the warranty beyond three years for an additional thirty-five dollars.

If you ask what sorts of damages the extended warranty covers, the associate might bombard you with an array of terms and stipulations. The associate might inform you; for example, that the warranty covers all damages outside of those caused by "normal use", or that the warranty extends beyond the limitations of the manufacturer's "lifetime warranty". The associate might also begin discussing particular damages such as water damage or sun damage. To determine whether an extended warranty may be a good investment, or even if an existing warranty applies to a malfunctioning device, a user should become familiar with some essential vocabulary, such as the ones mentioned as follows:

- **Manufacturer's warranty**: As indicated by the name, this warranty is provided by the manufacturer of a device. For most devices, the manufacturer's warranty provides for repair or replacement for a period of at least one year, and is often limited to a number of particular malfunctions. This warranty is usually intended as a method of ensuring customer satisfaction when a defective product manages to slip through a manufacturer's Quality Assurance department. Because most malfunctions are not due to a defective or faulty assembly, many consumers rarely utilize the manufacturer's warranty to repair and replace their devices. Two notable examples of a manufacturer's warranty in recent memory are Toyota's 2010 Accelerator Pedal recalls and Microsoft's 2009 warranty extension on its Xbox 360 games consoles.

- **Lifetime warranty**: This warranty is often, though not always, intended to cover a product for its "lifetime". Unfortunately, this term is problematic because the lifetime of a product is defined by the manufacturer or seller in the warranty's contract. For example, consider a consumer that purchases a mattress with a "Lifetime Warranty", and consider that this same mattress suffers severe damage eight years after its purchase. The warranty contract on the mattress may specify that the lifetime warranty is only applicable within a period of five years. In this case, the consumer would not be able to utilize the lifetime warranty to replace their product, because the damages occurred eight years after purchase. In fact, according to a 2010 Denver Post article, lifetime warranties are actually little more than a marketing tool because the supposed "lifetime" of a product is whatever the manufacturer or seller says it is (http://www.denverpost.com/business/ci_16380129).

- **Normal use/usage**: This is a common term used to categorize a wide array of damages and malfunctions. Specifically, normal use means any damages or malfunctions that are not due to defective or faulty assembly. For example, if a user drops his/her phone and the phone's screen is cracked as a result, this damage would be considered normal use. The same may be said for other common malfunctions or damages, such as scratched casing, sun damage, or water damage. Companies utilize normal use as a method of assessing whether certain damages are due to manufacturer error, and therefore whether the manufacturer's warranty applies. If a malfunction is determined to be the result of normal use, a manufacturer may refuse to replace or repair a user's device.

- **Extended warranty**: These are warranties which, as evidenced by the name, often "extend" beyond the duration of the manufacturer's warranty. In many cases, extended warranties also cover a wider variety of damages and malfunctions than manufacturers' warranties do. For example, an extended warranty on a television may cover a television for a period of three years, or two years longer than the duration of many manufacturers' warranties. Additionally, this extended warranty may cover all damages aside from theft or loss; if the user can bring the item in, they can utilize the warranty to obtain a replacement or repair. For the consumer, this means that extended warranties cover both manufacturers' errors and those damages which may fall under normal use. Extended warranties are almost always provided as an additional purchase, or add-on, for products. The most familiar product for which extended warranties apply for most consumers is on automobiles. Increasingly, however, extended warranties are being offered on devices ranging from televisions to smartphones and MP3 players.

- **Implied warranty**: Unlike the other terms previously listed, this type of warranty is unwritten and assumed. Many countries, including the United States, contain legal stipulations that any product must meet basic requirements, which are related to a product's claimed functionality. Essentially, this means that a product must possess the capabilities claimed by its seller or producer. For example, if an item is sold as a toothbrush, the item must be capable of performing the function of adequately brushing teeth. While this concept of implied warranty can be subject to interpretation, it is most useful for the average consumer as it pertains to false advertising accusations; does the product do what the seller or manufacturer said it can?

- **As is**: Products sold "as is" rarely, if ever, have warranties of any sort. These products are often used or worn products, which the seller may offer at a discounted price. Some sellers will offer extended warranties for as is products, but many consumers should be aware that these products are more prone to problems than brand new ones. One common as is product at many big-box stores are display models.

- **Cell phone insurance**: As it pertains to cell phones and smartphones, insurance is a type of warranty that may be considered as a type of extended warranty. Cell phone insurance is a product offered for an additional charge by many cellular providers. By purchasing the cell phone insurance, a user will be entitled to a replacement device should their device break or otherwise malfunction for various reasons. Some cell phone insurance products even guarantee replacement in the event that a device is stolen or lost.

In the United States, the **Uniform Commercial Code (UCC)** contains the legal stipulations for warranties and insurance on goods. For the curious, the complete text of the UCC is available on Cornell University's website at `http://www. law.cornell.edu/ucc/`.

Also, in the UK, consider the Sale of Goods ACT when caters for an "implied warranty"; refer to the following link:

`http://www.legislation.gov.uk/ukpga/1893/71/ pdfs/ukpga_18930071_en.pdf`

Navigating the web of warranties

Knowing which warranty applies to your particular device or malfunction is not always easy. Just as it is important to know which party to call for customer support issues, it is also important to know which, if any, warranty applies to your issue in the case of a broken or malfunctioning device.

Consider Toby's smartphone from the beginning of this chapter; he broke his device's screen by dropping it down the stairs. His device is unusable in its current state, and must be repaired or replaced. Toby ultimately decided to call the manufacturer, but he was unable to have the device replaced for free. This is because he dropped his phone down the stairs, and therefore the malfunction was due to "normal use" and would thus not be covered under the manufacturer's warranty. However, consider that Toby had decided to purchase some cell phone insurance from his cellular provider when he began his cellular contract over a year prior. Because he'd purchased this insurance, Toby could simply call his cellular provider and have them replace the device at no cost to him. Ask the company that is replacing the device if this device is new or a refurbished system.

The preceding scenario would appear to be fairly intuitive; Toby would choose to replace his device at no cost to himself because he had already purchased cell phone insurance. In some situations, however, this solution may not be so intuitive.

If Toby's device had broken due to faulty assembly, he could have decided to utilize the manufacturer's warranty to replace his device instead of his cell phone insurance. Depending on Toby's cell phone insurance contract, using the manufacturer's warranty could be preferable; this is because most cell phone insurance contracts contain stipulations or limitations. For example, Toby's cell phone insurance contract may specify that the insurance only applies to one device. If Toby were to decide to have his device replaced by the cellular provider instead of the manufacturer, he would no longer have cell phone insurance, as it would have expired after one use.

As you can see, deciding which warranty applies to your device can sometimes be complicated. For this reason, it is important to carefully read the warranty or insurance contracts for your devices. This is especially important because warranties can vary much from one device to another and one cellular provider to another. Before purchasing any sort of extended warranty or cell phone insurance, you should carefully compare the particulars of such warranty contracts with the manufacturer's warranty. In some cases, an extended warranty may provide little benefit above and beyond the manufacturer's warranty, and therefore may not be a wise investment.

Summing it up

As we become increasingly reliant upon our smartphones to conduct essential business tasks, maintaining and replacing these devices is also becoming more important. Should your device break, it is not always easy to know which party to contact to have your device replaced or repaired. While it is possible to simply call one party after another until your issue has been resolved, this is simply not a wise use of your time. By familiarizing yourself with the nature of technical support and warranties, you can reduce the amount of time between the manifestation of your error and having your functioning device in hand.

As BYOD becomes increasingly common, more employees will be expected to maintain or replace their malfunctioning devices. With the preceding steps and information, you should be able to resolve your issue in an effective and efficient manner.

Warranties

So far in this book we have defined the various types of warranties:

- Manufacturer's warranty
- Lifetime warranty
- Standard warranties
- Cell phone insurance

- Extended warranties
- Insurance

Our focus is on extended warranties and why you may want to invest or not invest into this type of warranty for your mobile device.

It is amazing that today you can purchase an extended warranty on almost any product. There are even companies that sell low priced snorkeling masks and will try to sell you an extended warranty. In general, extended warranties have a very high profit margin, so many companies will sell these warranties; even on toys.

Here is the scenario—you have an expensive mobile device and/or smartphone. You have obtained this device via a discount as part of a package that you purchased that comes with voice, data, and a device. One example is where you want to purchase a $500 device, but if you purchase the mobile service at the same time then you get the device for $150.00. Many companies will bundle services and devices together. At first glance this looks to be a really great deal. Now being a smart person you ask, "What if my device is damaged and/or stops working?" The person behind the counter now says, "We are here to help you, for just $19.99 a month you can get additional coverage if you damage your device." Also, the nice sales person tells you, "If you damage your device, you need to pay $500.00 to get a new one, unless you have our coverage." This story sound familiar?

Definitions

Before we get too far in this discussion let's define what type of smart device/phone you have. Your phone will fall into the following categories:

- A device for personal use only
- Work device provided by your company
- Bring Your Own Device (BYOD) for company use

Overall there would be little use to purchase any type of insurance/warranty on a device that is provided by your company; check with your company and ask in any case. The question you need to ask is, "If I drop my device in the Gulf of Mexico, who pays for it?" Also, your company may limit the ability for you to purchase an extended warranty, even if you wanted to spend your own money.

The scenario is where you (the consumer) are paying for your own device; for either your personal use or BYOD.

Before you spend any money on the extended warranty and/or insurance be sure and check to see what the manufacturer's warranty includes. Most mobile devices will include a one to two year warranty.

Types of extended warranties

There are several types of extended warranties, which include the following:

- **Verbal**: This is where the sales person tells you, "Sure that is covered!" Really? If I put my device in the driveway and back over it then your company will cover the repair? Always ask for the written details for any verbal promise.

- **Included**: Most to all devices have some type of warranty. There are rare cases where a device is warrantied for life.

- **Cost based on a recurring charge**: This is where you (the owner) will pay a monthly or yearly charge.

- **Embedded charge**: This is where a charge is added to your bill. This is very common and in some cases the consumer does not know they have been charged. There is also the issue that the consumer does not know they have this coverage.

Keep in mind that warranties will be specifically based on the manufacturer, the vendor that sells the product, and from what country the product is sold. We have just experienced this. We attempted to purchase a product from a company that is based in the United States. In this case we were physically located outside the USA in a Caribbean country. The seller told us that once we purchased the device that we would need to return the product back to the vendor in the USA in order to get service. In other words, once we walked out the door of the shop, we had *no* local warranty and/or support. The moral of this story is: just because you purchase a product from a known vendor, you may not get local service and every warranty can be different from country to country.

Extended warranty coverage

There are many different types of coverage; the following are a few examples:

- **Product defects**: Most products include some type of limited coverage if a device does not work. Most products will put a time limit on defect support; for example, 90 days or one year. Again, very few will provide lifetime support.

- **Damage**: This is a broad category. In some cases the device can be covered in the event that it is physically damaged. In a few rare cases, a device can be covered if it gets wet. There are also device options that can provide "damage" coverage. If you determine you need this, read the details carefully, most companies that sell these options provide a lot of limits in the event of physical damage or if the device has water damage.

- **Lost**: Overall this is mostly some type of insurance. Check with the vendor if these rules apply to your device. This book covers in detail the impact to you if your device is used for work. Many companies will execute a remote wipe if you report your device as lost. Always check with your company if your device is lost.

- **Software and applications**: As part of this process be sure and check to see if a bad application will be covered. In most cases all you need to do is to reset the device. But you need to read the details of your manufacturer's warranty and any extended warranty in any case. Also, if you jailbreak your device then the warranty may be void.

Extended warranty considerations

As we have noted in this section, it is up to you if you think you need to spend additional money on an extended warranty. Let's review some of the considerations on why you may want one:

- **Cost**: This is always an important issue. If the warranty is free, then you are home free. But are you? As we have noted the cost may be embedded into your monthly bill. Make sure that free is really free.

- **The written statement**: As with any contract be sure and get a copy and read it. One example is, "This warranty does not cover water damage." Also watch out for:

    ◦ What country are you getting the warranty in?

    ◦ What state? Yes, there are differences from state to state.

    ◦ **Uniform Commercial Code (UCC)**: This is a set of laws from the United States that describe the impact of implied warranties.

- **As-is**: Watch out for as-is devices; a good deal is not always a good deal.

- **A multiyear plan**: There are a lot of people who will purchase a multiyear mobile service plan. Along with these plans is an opportunity to purchase a device at a discount.

To purchase an extended warranty or not?

Now that you have the basic definitions, let's now guide you through the decision process. Review these points and make your own decision:

- Is your company providing the device for you? Will your company cover the replacement if the device is lost or damaged?

    ○ Be sure and ask up front. Your company may require that you sign a Mobile Acceptable Use Policy in order to receive a device. Be sure and read this document and then ask your company what the rules are if your device is lost or damaged.

- Is the warranty the same if you purchased the device online versus a physical store?

    ○ Be sure and check the details of a potential purchase if you get your device online. Also, determine the process on how to get your device replaced/repaired.

- If you purchase an extended warranty or insurance then is there a deductable?

    ○ Find out if there is a deductable charge that is applied if you try to get your device repaired or replaced. Be sure that you can add any deductable charges to the overall cost of your warranty changes.

- If you purchase an as-is device, is the warranty the same and/or can you purchase an extended warranty?

    ○ There are limits to warranties and as-is devices based on the UCC

- Does the manufacturer's warranty provide the coverage you need?

    ○ This is really the big question. At the end of the day you need to balance the coverage, the cost of the coverage, and your personal budget. Another important point is to read the terms and conditions of the base warranty as well as the extended warranty. It is OK to ask the sales person about what is covered, just also have the sales person show you the coverage in writing. Also, be sure and check the warranty on the battery. Ask if the manufacturer's warranty covers the battery during the life of the device and/or the warranty. If you are considering purchasing an extended warranty, consider the fact that you may be paying for a warranty on top of the manufacturer's warranty. Be sure and ask about the coverage time frame of the warranty. It is possible to purchase an extended warranty that covers the same time frame as the manufacturer's warranty. The overlap of coverage would not be cost effective.

- Is the warranty worth the paper it is printed on?
    - ° Another important question. Ask the sales person, "Who actually owns the warranty?" In some cases the warranty is not being provided by the company that manufactured the device. If the third-party company goes out of business, you cannot get your device repaired/replaced. Take the time to research the company that offers the warranty before you spend your money.

- How often do you change your device?
    - ° Some companies will provide a clause in the warranty that you can "upgrade" to a new device. Some people like to change a device as soon as there is a new feature every three months, in this case you may not want to sign up for a two-year warranty.

- Does your device break often?
    - ° Take a few minutes and check out your favorite Internet search engine. See how often small appliances need to be repaired. Consumer reports provide information on repair rates on a large range of devices. Check out http://www.consumerreports.org/cro/electronics-computers/resource-center/buying-electronics/overview/buying-electronics-ov.htm.

- Does your credit card offer better protection?
    - ° Some credit cards offer to double the length of the manufacturer's warranty. Check with your credit card company and see what they offer.

In a nutshell

As pointed out, it is up to you if you think you need to spend money to add a warranty, or insurance, to your device or smartphone. At the end of the day you need to make that decision. Use this summary to guide you:

- Companies make a lot of money from extended warranties; today's electronics do not break that much.

- In some cases an extended warranty is redundant to the manufacturer's warranty.

- Is the device a company-owned device? If so, ask your company before you try to purchase any type of insurance and/or warranty.

- Are you buying an extended warranty for peace of mind?

We do recommend that you review the data we provided and make your own decision.

Summary

In this chapter, we discussed how to get your device serviced in the event of a significant malfunction. Topics covered include the following:

- Bring Your Own Device (BYOD) and device malfunctions
- Service Level Agreements and how they matter to you
- Customer support systems: phone, SMS, or chat
- The three types of smartphone device malfunctions: hardware, operating system, and application
- Steps to take before calling customer support
- Steps to take while "on the line" with customer support
- Different types of warranty products, including extended warranties
- How to best determine which warranty applies to your malfunction

7

Baby Boomers, Teens, and Tweens

We have looked at managing your mobile device for ordinary usage, risks to your device and personal information, ways to protect them, and various types of support available to you if issues arise. Mobile devices have come a long way in a very short amount of time, from simple phones to fully functioning computers. The possibilities are almost endless. There are other, less obvious risks which may arise from using mobile devices. While they may never touch your life, it is important to be aware of them if you are responsible for minors or have family members or friends in the over-50 age group. In this chapter, we will look at some of the most important risks and developments.

A mobile device, by its nature, is usually small and portable. Small, portable things have a tendency to get lost. Shiny mobile devices are attractive to thieves, who can casually swipe them from a restaurant table or shopping counter as they walk by. The information stored for quick retrieval would be lost. Worse, it would be available to the thief for nefarious purposes. The same information, which is so helpful in reminding us how to contact people and where we need to be at a certain time, is also useful to a thief collecting personal information.

The thief could know where you are during your appointment, or where your children are. He or she could also know when you are not at home.

The thief can text your family members and friends with your mobile device, thus appearing to be you. There would be no vocal cues to warn the other person that you are not the person at the other end of the conversation. While some wording choices may provide clues, often the clues would not be noticed immediately. The family member or friend may provide the thief with personal or even sensitive information based on trusting you. The thief would be texting in order to obtain that information using social engineering techniques, with experience in doing so. Your contact would likely be unsuspecting and far less experienced, thus more likely to offer up the very information the thief is after.

The boom in baby boomers

Age has a funny way of changing bodies. The bones creak, the hearing starts to fail, the eyes lose some of their ability to focus, and the memory plays tricks by hiding, somewhere in the recesses of our minds, those things we have always known. We seek ways to compensate for these changes, such as pain medicines and hearing aids. Mobile devices can also provide compensation through built-in features that may not have been designed for that purpose, but can nevertheless prove helpful.

For example, many smartphones and tablets today allow you to expand the screen, thus increasing the size of the font and items displayed. This can be very helpful for eyes struggling to read normal-sized font. The devices also have an ever-expanding memory available for the user to save important information such as names, phone numbers, and appointments.

As more and more people reach the age 50 years and older, manufacturers of many types of products are finding it beneficial to target products to the needs of this age group. Mobile device manufacturers have been busy with that effort for quite a while. They have made available cell phones with large, easy-to-read number pads, and simple instructions (for people who are not used to technology). This effort will continue to grow in importance over the coming decades. Today, there are more people over the age of 60 years, than children under five years. By 2022, the number of people over 60 years will surpass 1 billion, an increase of about 200 million people since 2012 (http://www.guardian.co.uk/global-development/2012/oct/01/un-report-action-need-ageing-population).

The number of available features benefitting older people will continue to grow, whether through planning or through coincidence. Some features to look for: better coordination between hands-free earpieces and hearing aids, touch screens and key pads more compatible with shaking hands, and more apps targeting the interests of retired people. The device shown is one of the examples of a mobile phone with large font and buttons, making its use easier for people with poor eyesight or shaky hands.

Imagine the benefits of a substantial amount of memory in a small mobile device to a person whose memory is starting to fail. With a few taps on the screen, the device can offer-up reminders for next week's doctor appointments, ring an alarm each time a medicine needs to be taken, and even display the name and dosage of the medicine. Searching for a lost address book would be a thing of the past, because all contact information for family, friends, acquaintances, and business contacts would be at one's fingertips. For people who forget ATM PINs, e-mail IDs and passwords, and bank account information, the mobile device could be a handy place to store it all, for quick retrieval when needed.

There is an inherent risk with that idea. As mentioned previously, all of the information stored in the device could be available to the finder, if the device were lost or stolen. Extra precautions, such as password protection, would be needed to ensure that access to the information was restricted.

Colliding generations

We've seen it coming, the workplace collision of two generations with very different communication skills. We are already working on the cleanup, but probably missed the moment of impact. Can you recall when you first realized that the new college hire in your meeting was responding in a way foreign to the experienced staff? Perhaps you couldn't quite put your finger on what was different, or maybe you noticed the tempo was a bit off, a bit faster than usual. Maybe you noticed that the new college hire reacted to levels of management differently, or paid no attention to the hierarchy that is long revered as an integral part of the organization.

You may be asking yourself, "What does this have to do with the future of technology and protecting myself?" The answer is, "A lot".

People growing up in the second decade of the 2000s communicate electronically far more than only one generation prior (`http://www.educause.edu/research-and-publications/books/educating-net-generation/convenience-communications-and-control-how-students-use-technology`, `http://www.cellular-news.com/story/45544.php?ModPagespeed=noscript`). They not only communicate in person, but also via text, e-mail, and videoconferencing. On the positive side, they are able to remain in contact more often with more people simultaneously than their parents could. On the other hand, they are missing many valuable aspects of face-to-face communications and possibly even parts of the communications they are involved in due to multi-tasking.

In the late 2012, the New York Times revealed that the results of surveys focused on the attention span of students aged 8 to 18 years. Of the teachers surveyed, 90 percent noticed a marked decline in attention spans and the quality of students' work compared to students even a decade ago. The teachers largely blamed this on the students' increased exposure to technology, its entertainment value, and its impact on attention spans. One teacher remarked, "What's going to happen when they don't have constant entertainment?" Teachers have implemented several approaches for addressing these challenges, as follows:

- Adding more individual tutoring sessions
- Developing more dynamic and flexible teaching styles
- Coaching students on how to work through challenging assignments
- Using educational video games and digital presentations

(`http://www.nytimes.com/2012/11/01/education/technology-is-changing-how-students-learn-teachers-say.html?_r=0`) A technologist at HP stated that technology's quick interactions will be detrimental to focusing on the harder problems, and that we will probably see stagnation in many areas of technology, even social venues, such as literature (`http://mashable.com/2012/02/29/technology-effects-on-childrens-brains/`).

How does the shorter attention span tie to your business meeting? How is technology involved? The meeting requires concentration for an extended period of time, providing little drama (other than the occasional argument), and allowing only one person to act at a time. People reaching adulthood today grew up on technology that trained their brains to work in a contradictory environment. Meetings and the traditional work environment require long-term concentration, listening and absorbing verbal dialogue, and producing results that often take considerable time to develop. Today's technology reinforces instant results with drama. The challenges encountered by teachers in the classroom have migrated to the workplace.

Speaking of the younger generation...

A US study in the spring of 2012 confirmed the continued rise in cell phone ownership among minors. The percentage of high school students with cell phones, 85 percent, is not surprising, although finding almost the same percentage of ownership (83.5 percent) for middle schoolers is. The numbers continue to surprise as we go down a few grades, with fifth graders at 39 percent, fourth graders at 26.5 percent, and third graders at 19 percent. Third graders are usually nine years old; thus the study's findings show that one in five nine year olds carries a cell phone (http://news.cnet.com/8301-1023_3-57411576-93/one-fifth-of-third-graders-own-cell-phones/). This percentage will have even more meaning as we look at the corresponding risks children face due to mobile devices.

Cell phone ownership among the under-10 crowd in the UK is even higher than in the US with 33 percent owning a cell phone. One in 10 children under the age of 10 years owns an iPhone. Of the parents surveyed, 50 percent stated that they did not install parental controls on their child's phone (http://www.digitaltrends.com/mobile/survey-10-percent-of-uk-under-10s-have-an-iphone-a-third-have-a-cell-phone/). Children in most other European countries are less likely to carry cell phones; only 12 percent of children aged 9 years to 16 years are able to access the Internet via personally-owned mobile devices. Swiss children are an exception at 49 percent (http://phys.org/news/2012-09-children-switzerland-mobile-online.html). In Asia, children in the Philippines have an even higher percentage of cell phone ownership than Swiss children, with 66 percent of Filipino children aged 7 years to 14 years owning a cell phone (http://www.mobilemonday.net/reports/SEA_Report_2012.pdf).

PHOTO: FABRICE COFFRINI/AFP/GETTY IMAGES

Children carrying cell phones have the ability to instantly contact their parents, school staff, and friends. Yet, with so many children carrying mobile devices, it is important to recognize the corresponding risks and take steps to mitigate them.

Texting, sexting, and the Internet

Texting is a form of communication using short messages sent between mobile devices. Sexting is a form of texting which includes sexually explicit messages, photos, and videos. A child does not have to send a **sexually explicit text message (sext)** to receive one. In fact, the sender may not even know who is receiving the sext by simply entering any phone number, similar to prank calls on land-based phone lines. Depending on the age and personality of the child, the parents may not find out about the message, missing out on the opportunity to teach the child personal views on that type of content and ways to avoid it, if desired.

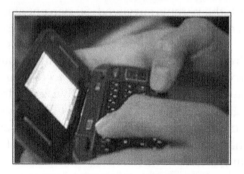

Children may also choose to be actively involved in sexting, sharing messages with a significant other or just friends. Recent surveys indicate that up to 40 percent of children have sexted and 20 percent have included nude or partially nude photos of themselves (http://www.thenationalcampaign.org/sextech/pdf/sextech_summary.pdf). Once such a photo is sent, the child has no control over where it ends up. The recipient is free to post the photo on any social networking or other website, including websites geared towards pornography. In addition, uploading images often assigns certain rights of the image to the service that the image is uploaded to. Once posted, it is almost impossible to remove it from public viewing. While it may be possible to have a photo removed from one website, the photo may have been downloaded to and exist on an unknown number of computers.

Children with mobile devices that allow Internet access have access to the full expanse of the Internet, unless limiting controls are put in place. Thus, a child has access to and could be exposed to sexually explicit content with or without intending to view such material. An innocent Internet search could produce unintended and explicit results. Adults can recognize and thus avoid material that does not align with personal preferences; however, a child may not even be aware that such material exists or understand its potential harm to minors. A child may view the content, seek out more, and even share the material with other children, all without the knowledge or consent of parents.

Commercial products exist which allow a parent to control the content that a child's phone can receive and what the child can do with the phone. The controls can be set more stringent when the child is younger and loosened up as the child ages. For example, on most devices, parents can control Internet access, downloading options, and texting. In addition, parents can choose to disable geo-tagging on devices to prevent unwanted tracking of their children (`http://staysafeonline.org/stay-safe-online/mobile-and-on-the-go/mobile-parental-controls`). Unfortunately, not all parents activate these controls.

Products are only a part of the equation, however parents should actively train children on mobile device safety in an age-appropriate manner, repeating the training regularly as the children mature. Training should include rules on sharing personal information, such as name, age, address, family information, and future plans. An additional safety feature that can be implemented on a child's mobile device is a content filtering tool such as SafeSearch by Google. This tool screens results from search requests and only allows the display of results passing the safety filter settings.

Strangers and dangers

Strangers can contact children through mobile devices without parents or teachers being aware. Adults can also be contacted; however, the potential for harm to children is much greater. If a stranger contacts an adult wanting to chat, offering a free ride in a nice car, or suggesting a meeting somewhere, the adult will probably decline. Experience will tell the adult to question the person's honesty and motives. Children develop the ability to differentiate between truth and lies as they mature. Add to children's inexperience, the anonymity provided by technology and a person can pretend to be friendly, kind, fun, rich, anything desired. Mix in a home life of abuse or neglect and the temptation for loving attention may be too much for a child to turn down. Pedophiles and other predators know this and use it to their advantage to chat with children, develop relationships with them, and eventually convince the children to meet in person.

If this seems more like fantasy than reality, look at the 2010 case in California in which a 40 year old man posed as a friendly 16 year old boy in order to talk to teenage girls via a cell phone. He managed to convince the girls, as he was friendly and initiated sexting with them, talking several of them into sending him semi-nude photos. Once he had the photos he would threaten to post them on the Internet if the girls didn't provide him with the cell phone numbers of their friends.

The training mentioned previously should include discussion on ways to handle messages and phone calls from strangers. Similar to the long-standing rule of, "Don't talk to strangers", "Don't text with strangers", should be taught and enforced. Human nature causes us to want to believe that it could not happen in our family, but that is wishful thinking best saved for winning the lottery.

And unlimited damage

None of the dangers described previously have a greater impact than cyberbullying. Before children and teens had practically unlimited access to the Internet and social networking sites, bullying could only be done with limited scope. The taunting had to be done in person, in writing, or over the phone. The audience was small or nonexistent. The Internet and widespread use of cell phones by minors changed all that. One teen or child could torment another publicly and permanently.

Cyberbullying is defined as, "a young person tormenting, threatening, harassing, or embarrassing another young person using the Internet or other technologies, such as cell phones" (http://www.dosomething.org/tipsandtools/11-facts-about-cyber-bullying). Like other items posted on the Internet, cyberbully posts last indefinitely, as can the scars produced. The content of cyberbullying can range from brief taunts posted once to constant lies intended to destroy a child's reputation. The goals of cyberbullies range from personal entertainment to severe harm.

How serious is cyberbullying, and how widespread? According to DoSomething. org, over 40 percent of minors in America have been the victims of cyberbullying, and 25 percent have been victimized more than once. By 2010, two-thirds of the states had passed laws addressing cyberbullying (http://www.ncsl.org/issues-research/educ/cyberbullying.aspx). And the news has unfortunately included stories of children suffering serious consequences from cyberbullying or even committing suicide to escape its incessant torture.

How can a parent or guardian detect cyberbullying is occurring? Kidshealth.org offers the following signs to look for:

- Signs of emotional distress during or after using the Internet or the phone
- Being very protective or secretive of their digital life
- Withdrawal from friends and activities
- Avoidance of school or group gatherings
- Slipping grades and "acting out" in anger at home
- Changes in mood, behavior, sleep, or appetite

If bullying is suspected, either physically or via technical means, speak with the child. Get help for the child, either through the school counselor or a professional therapist. But be sure to respect the child's need for privacy. The same steps should be taken for children perpetrating cyberbullying. Often, they are acting out due to emotional issues and need help to resolve those issues before they become permanent behavior patterns. Both the bully and the victim can suffer long-term effects, so prompt and effective help is necessary.

Summary

In this chapter, we looked at some benefits and risks for older people using mobile devices. While the devices can provide benefits, they can also open the door to the loss of personal information. We also reviewed technology's impact on children and young adults, and steps parents can take to make mobile devices safer for minors. Impacts to the workplace environment were discussed, focusing on technology's effects on the various working generations. Finally, we looked at the cruelty of and damage done by cyberbulling. The next chapter will deal with the steps to be carried out after knowing that your device is hacked.

8

Getting Your Life Back After You've Been Hacked

By following the advice contained in this book, you will be able to reduce the likelihood of your device or information getting hacked. However, it is important to remember that hackers may still, despite our best intentions, be successful in their attempts at hacking our devices. Every user should prepare a list of steps, phone numbers, and device information in the event that a device or information is hacked. With such a list in hand, a user will reduce the time and frustration entailed in containing the damage and getting life back on track after an incident.

This chapter will show:

- What is included in a device profile and why this is important to you
- Why backups are important
- What to do if you have been hacked
- A checklist of what you should do if your device is hacked/lost
- What to do if your device is lost

Device profiles

Every mobile device has a built-in profile. These profiles include information about the device, the device configuration, and your personal configurations. In effect the profile is the brain of your device. If the device is corrupted and/or hacked, the profile can be destroyed. This chapter will show an example of an Apple profile and an Android profile.

If the profile is not working, the device will not work. Information included in a device profile can include:

- Your name
- The device ID numbers (detailed in other chapters)
- Cell phone number (not all devices have cell numbers)
- The last time the device was used and in some cases if the device has been backed-up
- Messaging profiles
- Applications installed

These are example screenshots and can change between each release of Android and/or iOS.

The Apple profile

As with most phones/devices, Apple products have a profile. The Apple profile is found under **Settings**. An example is as follows:

You will note that the preceding screenshot shows that a software update is needed.

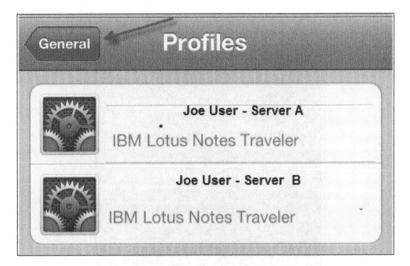

If you need to process a hard reset, you can protect yourself by creating and managing a backup of your device. The method to back up and restore a device can depend on what type of device you have. The following are its examples.

Apple backup

Apple provides the ability to backup and restore your device via iCloud and iTunes. This is mostly an automated process that you can use to back up most data on your iPhone or iPad. The backup normally includes:

- The phone profile
- Applications
- Music
- Videos
- Books
- Pictures

The Android profile

As with an Apple device, Android also has profiles. Android profiles can be found in the **Settings** section.

A sample profile from an Android device is as follows:

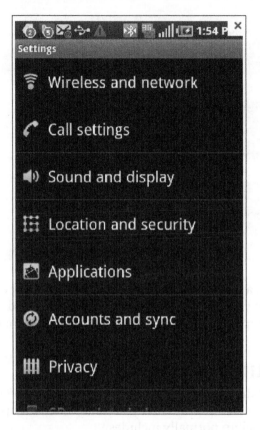

Android backup

One easy method to execute a backup for your Android phone is via the **Mobile Backup & Restore Tool** available at https://play.google.com/store/ apps/details?id=com.trendmicro.backupandrestore&hl=en. This application will provide the same type of backup that the Apple iTunes application will provide, including:

- The phone profile
- Applications
- Music
- Videos
- Books
- Pictures

Other Android backup tools include:

- Mobile Backup II available at `https://play.google.com/store/apps/details?id=mobilehome.backup&hl=en`
- Trend Micro Mobile Backup and Restore available at `http://www.trendmicro.com/us/home/products/mobile-solutions/online-backup-restore/index.html`

Have you been hacked?

Let's review some important points from *Chapter 5, Protecting Your Mobile Devices*. It is very important for you to recognize if you have been hacked. Believe it or not, many users remain unaware that their device or information has been compromised until significant damage has been done. This is confirmed from a study that Symantec executed in 2012. This study identified the following important points:

- 55 percent of end users are not sure if their device is clean of virus or malware
- About 33 percent of end users don't know how to protect themselves online
- 49 percent of the end users surveyed did not understand if there is a virus or malware on their computer based on the fact that the computer may be running slow

This survey can be found at `http://now-static.norton.com/now/en/pu/images/Promotions/2012/cybercrimeReport/2012_Norton_Cybercrime_Report_Master_FINAL_050912.pdf`.

Here's a list of signs that may indicate your device has been hacked:

- **Deleted or installed files**: If files have disappeared or appeared that you did not delete or install, this may be a sign that your device has been compromised.
- **Photos**: Check to see if there are unusual photos or videos that may have been removed or added to your device.
- **Receiving strange text**: Strange texts with abstract symbols may indicate that your device has been hacked. If you have received such texts, power off your device immediately. Do not power it back on until you have addressed the problem. See the next sections for details.
- **Sent e-mails**: Check regularly the sent items for text and e-mails to keep a check on what is being sent from your device.
- **Rejected e-mails**: If you see a lot of rejected e-mails, this can be an indication of an issue with your device.

- **Outgoing phone calls, e-mails, or text**: If your friends have received e-mails, calls, or text which you did not send, this should be considered a sign that your device or profiles have been hacked. Examine your outgoing mail, phone call, and text folders for unauthorized communications.

- **Evidence of any unfamiliar activity on your device**: Unfortunately, sometimes the only evidence that your device has been hacked is strange or unexplainable activity. Have you been experiencing sudden drops in service in places in which you normally receive a strong signal? Have your settings changed without you having changed them? It is important that you, as a user, not ignore any strange activity on your device: if it seems strange, then investigate. Several sites will notify you if your password has been changed; if you receive an e-mail that your password has changed and if you did not change it, you have an issue with your device. Another point is that you should know what is listed in your device profile settings. If you see that your profile has changed, you may have malware on your device.

Knowing the difference – device hacks, profile hacks, or both

Having recognized strange behavior, it is then important to determine the exact nature and extent of the vulnerability. If your profile has been compromised, and you did not use the same credentials for multiple accounts, the solution may be relatively simple; change your credentials for the compromised account. If, on the other hand, you believe that your device has been compromised, the solution may entail additional steps.

A general rule of thumb for distinguishing between the two is whether the strange behavior occurs within one application, or if the strange behavior seems spread out over multiple applications or activities. For example, are your friends receiving both strange text and strange e-mails? Have multiple apps begun to malfunction or demonstrate strange behavior? If so, the nature of the hack may be related to your device and not limited to one profile. In such a case, the likelihood that your profile information has also been hacked increases, as a compromised device means that all applications accessed through the device may have been compromised.

In the event of a hack

You've determined to the best of your ability that your device has been hacked. At the very least, you've determined that your device is demonstrating behavior that you cannot otherwise explain. The following are the steps you should take depending on the particulars of your hack.

The device type (BYOD or the corporate device)

Depending on whether your device is a **Bring Your Own Device (BYOD)** or is owned by your employer, the steps which you take should be similar. If you own the device, you may just initiate a device reset. Every device has the ability for a basic reset. In most cases, this will remove all the data and applications and place the device into an original setup state.

For example:

- **Apple**: `http://support.apple.com/kb/HT1430`

  Apple also has on online assistant at `http://www.apple.com/support/iphone/assistant/`

- **Samsung**: `http://www.hard-reset.com/`

Be sure and check each vendor for their support sites.

BYOD

If your device is a Bring Your Own Device (BYOD) or is owned by your employer, the steps which you should take may vary. In most cases, the company will instruct you to a specific help desk number. The company will inform you of what to do next depending on their policies.

If your device is a BYOD, you will likely need to address the problem as if it was a personal device. In addition, you will also need to inform your employer of the hack; depending on your employer's policies, they may decide to conduct a partial or complete wipe of your device to contain potential damage. Check with your company regarding the rules if a device can be wiped. The Mobile Acceptable Use policy can describe if this can happen to you. If a wipe is executed, it is possible that the Mobile Device Management tool can execute the wipe.

If your device is BYOD, you will need to consider whether your error is a hardware, operating system, or application malfunction. Depending on your device, the type of malfunction you are experiencing will determine which party can assist you. If the error is a hardware malfunction, you will likely need to contact your device's manufacturer. If your error is an operating system or user interface malfunction, you will likely need to contact the operating system's developer. In some cases, as with iOS devices, the manufacturer and operating system developer are the same party; with iOS it is Apple. However, with other devices such as Windows Phones, the manufacturer and operating system developers are usually different parties. One example is Nokia Lumia. In this case, you would contact Nokia for operating system issues and not Microsoft. Another example would be the Samsung Galaxy S3, where you would contact Samsung for any operating system issues and not Google. The final type of error, application malfunctions, would require you to contact the application's developer. By knowing which party to contact, you can reduce the amount of time it takes to resolve your issue. Be sure and ask how to get help when you purchase your device.

Once you know which party to contact, it is important that you prepare some essential information before picking up the phone. You should prepare any relevant account information so that you can easily access it for purposes of personal identification. You should also familiarize yourself with your device's warranty information, as it may allow you to obtain a replacement or repaired device at no personal cost. Finally, you should be prepared to describe your device's malfunction in detail.

Once on the phone, it is important to remain proactive in solving your issue; it is your responsibility to verify that your issue is solved before you hang up the phone. You should take the time to carefully answer every question the customer support representative asks you; answering even seemingly unnecessary questions may reveal important information about your malfunction. When describing your malfunction to the representative, do not "skip" even apparently rudimentary steps such as powering on your device or entering your password. By including all steps, you can ensure that the representative has an accurate understanding of your malfunction. Finally, do not allow the representative to disconnect your call until you have verified that your malfunction is resolved by testing your device numerous times.

In the event that your device needs to be repaired or replaced, you should familiarize yourself with the specifics of any warranty products that you have purchased, as well as the manufacturer's warranty for your device. It is your responsibility to understand which warranties apply to your device. Pay careful attention when numerous warranties apply, such as when your malfunction is covered by both a manufacturer's warranty and an extended warranty. Depending on the specifics of your malfunction and warranties, it may be more beneficial to utilize one type over another.

Who to contact

As discussed earlier, regardless of whether your device is a BYOD or owned by your employer, you should contact your employer if you use your device to conduct company business. In addition to your employer, you will likely also need to contact at least one of a number of additional parties to address the issue.

If your device is still under warranty, you should contact your device's manufacturer. Depending on the nature of your hack, they may be able to provide you with a replacement device.

You should also contact your service provider. Depending on the nature and extent of the hack, you may need to change your phone number or account credentials. If you have purchased insurance from your provider, you may also be entitled to a replacement device should the current one be damaged beyond repair.

Finally, you will need to consider whether or not to contact additional parties depending on the sort of information which you believe may have been compromised. This includes, but is not limited to, your personal bank, social networking hosts, and e-mail provider. Any application or profile, which you accessed through your device, may have been compromised, and you may therefore need to contact those providers who manage each account.

To wipe or not to wipe – partial or complete

Depending on the specifics of your issue, you may need to remotely wipe your device. If the device was company-owned, this decision may be made by your employer and will not require your input. If the device was a BYOD, the decision to wipe may still be covered under your employer's BYOD acceptable use policies (example explained in *Appendix D*, *Mobile Acceptable Use Policy Template*). In some cases, employers may decide to wipe company data from compromised BYOD devices as a matter of policy.

In the event that your employer has no policy on whether or not to wipe compromised BYODs, the decision will fall upon you as to the best course of action. Some important questions to consider when deciding whether or not to wipe your device are:

- Did your device contain sensitive company or personal data?
- Did you use your device to access corporate or personal accounts?
- Have you lost access to your device due to it being stolen or lost?
- Do have you have good reason to believe that your issue is a hack rather than a simple malfunction?

If the answer to any of the above questions is *Yes*, then you may wish to conduct a partial or full wipe.

The decision to partially or completely wipe your device will depend on whether you wish to access your device in the future. Because a complete wipe will often render the device unusable or restored to factory settings, you will lose all data contained on the device. Losing all data is just that, you will lose your music, photos, and any stored files. In the event that the device is already unusable due to a complete hack, due to loss, or theft, a complete wipe may be the preferable course of action.

What to do and when to do it – a list in the event that you've been hacked

Below is a chart which you should fill out for personal use in the event that your device has been hacked or otherwise compromised. The following table also works if your device is lost. By filling out the following information, a user may reduce the difficulty entailed in collecting such information later. For example, if your device is stolen or lost, you may be unable to easily retrieve certain device-specific information (serial number, model number, and so on). Additionally, by having such information readily available, you will be able to decrease the time between discovering your device that has been compromised and resolving the issue.

Keep a list of essential applications (in case the device is wiped), and know where to locate serial numbers, encryption keys, and account codes for key applications (in case they need to be reinstalled). Immediately check your bills and request your latest credit card statements.

[Never create a list of personal credentials such as account numbers or passwords. Doing so will increase the risk that your credentials will be compromised.]

Issue	What to do	Relevant information
Lost or misplaced device	• Call your employer • Call your device service provider • Request a partial or complete device wipe • Change credentials for all accounts accessed by device	• Employer's Phone: _____ • Service Provider's Phone: _____ • Device Serial Number: _____ • Account Credentials: (Do not write down)

Issue	What to do	Relevant information
Hacked account (e-mail, social networking, bank)	• Call account provider • Change credentials • Assess which other accounts may have been compromised • Change credentials for additional compromised accounts	• Bank's Support Phone: ——————— • E-mail's Support Phone: ——————— • Social Networking's Support Phone: ——————— • Additional Account Support Phone: ——————— • Account Credentials: (Do not write down)
Unauthorized outgoing calls or texts	• Turn off device • Call service provider • Return device to service provider location • Change credentials for all accounts accessed by device	• Service Provider's Phone: ——————— • Service Provider's Location Address: ———————
Hacked or malfunctioning application	• Call the application's developer support line • Identify who you need to call if you have an operating system issue • Determine whether security risk is limited to the application or has spread to other applications and services • Contact service provider to determine extent of security risk • Call additional parties as necessary • Change credentials for all accounts accessed by device	• Application Developer's Phone: ——————— • Application Developer's Phone (Additional): ——————— • Service Provider's Phone: ———————

Summing it up

These are the steps that you, as a user, can take in the event of a hack. Most importantly, each user should be aware of the steps to take depending upon the exact nature of the security risk. By preparing a list tailored for each type of malfunction or hack, you can more efficiently resolve any security compromises.

The second primary component to resolving a mobile security compromise relates to whether a device is a BYOD, an employer-owned device, or a personal device. If it is either a BYOD or an employer-owned device, the employer may enforce a policy of conducting partial or complete wipes of the device to protect corporate data.

While undesirable, a successful hack does not necessarily incur significant damage to your device or personal data. By contacting the correct parties and by understanding the extent of a hack, you can often contain much of the damage or restore the information. By filling out the preceding list, you, as a user, are better prepared in the event of an incident.

Be sure and back up or document your profile settings and/or unique profile settings. One important area to make sure you identify is how to reconnect back to your mail or corporate mail system.

Summary

In this chapter, we discussed:

- What to do in the event of a hack
- The difference between device hacks and profile hacks
- Whom to contact in the event of a hack or a lost/damaged device
- Partial wipes and complete wipes
- Your checklist in the event of a hack or a lost/damaged device

A
IBM Notes Traveler

The delivery of electronic messaging and other services to mobile devices has evolved greatly in the past two decades. Initially, the delivery of mail, calendar, and contact information was limited to desktop synchronization with the device. The delivery of *over-the-air* services was limited greatly through proprietary devices such as the Blackberry and the Blackberry Enterprise Server technology. As mobile device technology evolved, the expansion of devices and varying operating systems has driven providers of electronic messaging services to expand offerings to allow for the use of varied devices to deliver services.

The services that were provided initially were limited and required proprietary server technology such as Good Technology to deliver a usable electronic messaging, calendar, and contact client with functional security. One example of this security capability is the ability to remove corporate sensitive information (wipe) from the devices in case they were stolen or lost. To help customers with mobile access, vendors of messaging systems, such as IBM and Microsoft, began to introduce technology to deliver information to the devices. The IBM approach was to add a service to the Domino Server offering to provide the messaging resources to non-Blackberry devices, such as iPhone, Android, or Windows Mobile.

The IBM Notes Traveler service was introduced as an add-on to the base IBM Domino server product. Initially, the technology was focused on delivering electronic messaging, calendar, and contact services to iOS devices. As the technology matured, the IBM Notes Traveler service expanded its offering and now offers a fully functioning environment, including the introduction of a standalone client for Android devices to ensure compatibility across vendors.

The architectural design of the IBM Notes Traveler service

The IBM Notes Traveler service has remained an add-on component to the IBM Domino server. This has allowed for the development of the service and delivery of modifications outside the normal delivery schedule of updates to the IBM Domino Server technology. This flexibility has allowed for the expansion of the IBM Notes Traveler services to include Mobile Device Management functionality such as a partial wipe, which allows for the removal of only corporate-based information without impacting the personal data that exists on the device. Another new feature is high availability through leveraging an Enterprise Database Architecture. This expansion continues to allow for the flexibility to meet the changing requirements, operating systems, and device changes of the mobile marketplace.

Determining the correct deployment approach

The IBM Notes Traveler service is a robust client that continues to expand and deliver flexibility for corporate environments leveraging the IBM Notes and Domino technology. The service can provide a robust environment that is flexible in deployment and delivery, but it is important that the organization determines the security and architectural model before deployment to ensure that all standards and requirements are met. Additionally, it is important to understand if third-party resources such as reverse proxy or enterprise device management exist within the infrastructure. The IBM Notes Traveler environment can leverage other tools that exist, but a thorough understanding of the requirements to leverage these assets is required.

Review of the IBM Notes Traveler Server

The IBM Notes Traveler service is a component of the IBM Domino Server technology that allows for the communication and synchronization of mail, calendar, scheduling, and contact information to Apple iOS, Android, Windows Mobile, and Nokia devices running the legacy OS. The IBM Notes Traveler Server codebase has been split out from the core Domino server to allow for flexibility in deployment and development of the product. The Traveler server is installed in the environment on an IBM Domino Enterprise Server and configured to provide support not only for communication and synchronization of the information from the messaging environment, but also to provide some **Mobile Device Management (MDM)** capabilities that allow for the management of devices attaching to the service. The following sections will provide an overview of the Traveler environment along with the current capabilities within the product. For a complete set of current product capabilities and information, please refer to `http://www-01.ibm.com/software/lotus/products/notes/traveler.html`.

Overview of different clients

The IBM Notes Traveler configuration differs based on the mobile device that is being leveraged by the end user. The Traveler environment leverages the native mail, calendar, scheduling, and contact information clients on Apple iOS, Windows Mobile, and Nokia devices (legacy Nokia technology in addition to the new focus for the technology based on the Windows Mobile platform). The Android devices leverage a proprietary client developed by IBM to provide consistency throughout the environment. As a result of different implementations across the providers of Android-based mobile devices, the IBM Notes Traveler development team has developed a client that is deployed on the end user's device. The goal is to provide the required consistency across the end user community to allow for a simplified management and support organizations throughout the environment.

Access to the IBM Notes Traveler Servers

There are a number of configurations for the IBM Notes Traveler Server environment. This section will review the communication from devices to the infrastructure, along with the different topologies that can be deployed within the environment to provide support for the IBM Notes Traveler Server(s). It is important to note that the size of the organization, the demand on resources, security, and the requirements for redundancy/high availability will all significantly impact the final deployment configuration.

Communication to the devices

The standard configuration for the IBM Notes Traveler Server is to have devices connect to the infrastructure via HTTP or HTTPs. Alternatively, with Nokia, Windows, and Android devices (not Apple iOS), a **Short Message Service** (**SMS**) message can be sent to the devices to alert them that there is information on the server to initiate a pull from the device.

The IBM Notes Traveler Server connects to the IBM Domino servers through the standard NRPC 1352; so when planning the topology for the Traveler environment, it is important to understand where the servers are placed within the environment and how the end users will be accessing the servers. The largest concern is typically over the security of the environment and adherence to internal security policies on what can be placed in the DMZ and how access from the external environment, through the DMZ and to the internal environment, is accomplished. The environment may already have variances for the opening of ports or the placement of specific servers.

Location of the IBM Notes Traveler Servers

The IBM Notes Traveler Server can be located on the IBM Domino Mail Servers or on a secondary server running the IBM Notes Traveler services. If the IBM Notes Traveler Server is located on the mail servers, the service will reference `names.nsf` on the server directly. If the IBM Notes Traveler service is located on a secondary server, the IBM Notes Traveler service will look up the mail server and the file on the local, `names.nsf`, and redirect to the appropriate server to fulfill the request. In some situations, to add an additional level of security, the IBM Notes Traveler Server can be established in another domain to allow for the isolation of `names.nsf` for IBM Notes Traveler specific configurations and updates or for more security. If the IBM Notes Traveler Server is established in its own domain, the environment will not contain the required mail server and file information. Therefore, the IBM Notes Traveler Server will require the establishment of Domino Directory Assistance to allow for the lookups. It is important that the administrator leverage the default traveler policies to ensure that consistency is maintained across the environments. Additionally, this will enforce the policies for any user that connects to the IBM Notes Traveler Server.

Location of the mail servers

The demand on the overall environment, mail, and Traveler servers, is dependent on the distance that the servers are located from each other in terms of network. It is not necessary to have Traveler servers located on each mail server or in each location that mail servers are supported, but the distance between the two will impact the delay in delivering information to the devices. This delay can cause a perception among the user community that the servers are not performing at optimal levels. Locating multiple servers within the infrastructure to reduce the distance between the traveler and mail servers should be given great consideration, particularly when regional geographical conditions exist.

Connection methodologies to the Traveler servers

While there are a number of different configurations that can be deployed with Traveler; the main configurations are through VPN technology, reverse proxy, or direct connection. Each topology has implications on costs and security for the environment; it is important to understand the placement of your Domino Servers, reverse proxy/VPN architecture along with the corporate security policies that are in place to ensure that the correct method is instituted. The following is a short overview of the architectures that are commonly put in place within the environment.

Direct connection

The simplest configuration of the traveler environment is a direct connection to the Traveler server in the DMZ. This allows for the mobile devices to access the Traveler server over HTTPs or HTTP and the Traveler Server will access the Domino Servers through the firewall over NRPC Port 1352. This configuration can be viewed as the least secure, as the Traveler Server is sitting in the DMZ and is accessible directly from the Internet. The following is a simplified example of this architecture:

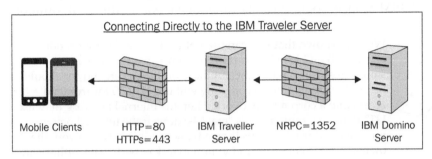

Reverse proxy

Deploying the IBM Notes Traveler environment leveraging a reverse proxy provides more security within the environment, although it adds another layer of complexity. This allows for the mobile devices to access the reverse proxy over HTTPs and then the reverse proxy maintains the access through to the Traveler Server over an HTTPs connection. The IBM Notes Traveler Server then will access the Domino Servers over NRPC 1352. In this configuration, the Domino Servers sit behind the firewall and the transaction is secured through the environment. Although the IBM Notes Traveler environment has only been tested against IBM Lotus Mobile Connect 6.1, IBM WebSphere Edge Server 6.1, and IBM Tivoli Access Manager 6.0, the environment is flexible and should leverage the current reverse proxy configuration deployed in your environment; it is encouraged that you test the environment to ensure complex fidelity.

IBM Mobile Connect

IBM Mobile Connect (formerly IBM Lotus Mobile Connect), known as IMC, provides a full-featured wireless VPN. This software provides the ability to send mobile data securely end-to-end through an enterprise. One of the features that IMC brings to the table is the ability to secretly access enterprise applications via a single frontend. Specific features include:

- Mobile device management into the enterprise — in particular access to Traveler

- Any device access into **iNotes** (IBM iNotes, also known as **DWA**)

- iNotes is sometimes accessed through a device known as **IBM Mobile Connect (IMC)**

IBM Sametime client for mobile device access is provided by the IBM WebSphere Proxy Server and not directly via IBM Mobile Connect.

The next diagram shows a reverse proxy environment that your company can implement. IBM Mobile Connect can be an optional part of this configuration.

 We have shown that you can use both HTTP (traffic that is not encrypted) and HTTPS (traffic that is encrypted). There is not a simple answer on when each of these protocols can and/or should be used. In some cases a company will use HTTPS for frontend access into a corporate network. Then the internal network may use HTTP (not encrypted). This "may" be done if the internal network is considered trusted. This is an advanced topic between you, the owner of your network, and your network experts. The authors do recommend that if in doubt, use HTTPS.

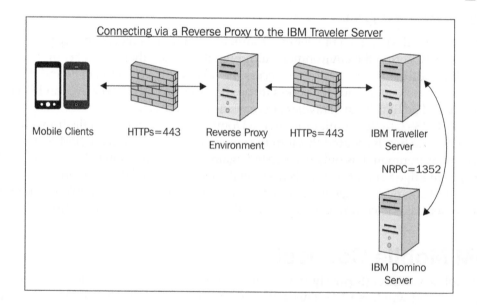

Connecting via a Reverse Proxy to the IBM Traveler Server

Mobile Clients   HTTPs=443   Reverse Proxy Environment   HTTPs=443   IBM Traveller Server

NRPC=1352

IBM Domino Server

VPN connection

Deploying the IBM Notes Traveler environment leveraging a **Virtual Private Network (VPN)** environment allows for the device to access all elements of the network through a single communication channel. The VPN connectivity should work for all devices, and it should be noted that the VPN service on the iOS devices are required to be started and managed by the end user manually, and this could cause connection delays due to the lack of connection to the IBM Notes Traveler Server. The IBM Notes Traveler Server will allow for access to the servers and will treat the connection as if it were native on the network; therefore, it is recommended to deploy the VPN configuration leveraging HTTP to minimize the duplication of providing security both through the VPN connection and the HTTPS connection. The IBM Notes Traveler Server then will access the Domino Servers over NRPC 1352. In this configuration, the Domino Servers sit behind the firewall and the transaction is secured through the VPN technology or HTTPS if required or configured. Since the IBM Notes Traveler Server is separated from the VPN connection technology, there is no requirement for a specific product to be used or tested (it should be noted that the IBM Lotus Mobile Connect client is entitled within the IBM Domino environment on a per-user basis; please refer to the IBM Lotus Mobile Connect product information for more information), although it is to encouraged that you test the environment to ensure complex fidelity.

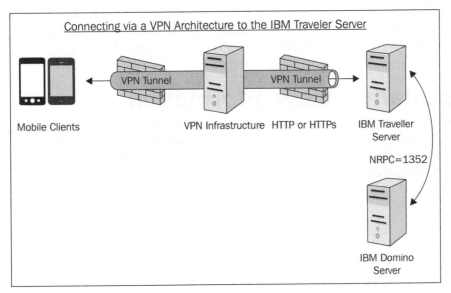

VPN Connection to the IBM Notes Traveler Server

Establishing appropriate security settings

The deployment of the IBM Notes Traveler Server in the environment can create new security considerations that have not existed with Mobile Device Management in the past, the Blackberry Enterprise Server was a very hardened and secure environment that required lock-down from the server and the device. As the shift is occurring to allow flexibility in devices, the establishment of strong security policies allows for flexibility on ownership of the device and continue to meet the corporate security requirements. The IBM Notes Traveler Server environment is configured to allow for a consistent deployment of security settings across the environment through the default device settings document located in the Traveler administration database. This policy document is designed to meet the standard security and device control settings that are required within an environment. If greater flexibility is required for specific users or groups of users, the deployment of security policies to differing groups in the environment, the administration of the environment can leverage Traveler Security policy settings. Both sets of security documents allow for the establishment of general polices in addition to device-specific settings.

The IBM Notes Traveler service meets the requirements for delivering messaging information from an IBM Domino environment to mobile devices without the need for additional software or services unless required to meet specific security policies. Included in *Appendix B, Mobile Device Management*, is a review of the requirements for mobile device management when addressing delivering technology to mobile devices. The IBM Notes Traveler Service provides a robust set of MDM features and can provide a secure environment that meets the requirements of today.

Important review information

The IBM Domino Traveler service is updated periodically throughout the year, but also provides hotfixes to address issues and concerns with the product. It is important to refer to the product documentation to ensure that the latest information related to the product is being leveraged within the environment.

Licensing information for IBM Notes Traveler

IBM Notes Traveler is not considered a standalone product that can be purchased from IBM; it is entitled through the appropriate licensing of the client environment. The entitlement for the IBM Traveler environment is obtained through proper maintenance of the IBM Domino Enterprise or Messaging CAL (this includes express and Complete Enterprise Options) licensing model. Each end user that has an active subscription and support for either the Enterprise or Messaging version of the IBM Domino CAL has the ability to access the resources provided by the IBM Domino Servers running the service. As the deployment of the IBM Notes Traveler service on the Domino Server may be dependent on a more advanced release of the IBM Domino server code, active subscription and support would be required on the IBM Domino Server. Please contact your IBM Collaboration Services representative to ensure that you are properly licensed to deploy the IBM Notes Traveler product within your environment.

New in IBM Notes Traveler IBM is planning on releasing IBM Notes Traveler in the first half of 2013. As the mobile market place changes and grows, IBM has tried to evolve the Traveler product to meet the needs of users. The IBM Notes Traveler 9 release is slated to include a new service for Apple and Android devices to handle the management of synchronizing to-dos between the devices and the Domino Server, additional support for Windows 8 and Blackberry 10 devices, and expanded support for server-based operating systems.

The new to-do functionality will allow Apple and Android devices to perform the following functions: review to-dos, complete to-dos or remove them entirely, create new to-dos, organize to-dos into lists, and sync attachments as part of to-do data. To perform the synchronization of the data with the Apple iOS will require that the end users download a new free IBM Notes Traveler to-do application from the App store.

The new IBM Notes Traveler 9 will also include support for Windows Phones (7.5, 7.8, and 8) along with Windows RT support. The support for the Windows RT environment is slated to be through the exchange account facility on the device. The initial release of support will contain limited functionality around managing the calendar facility. The Blackberry 10 device can be leveraged in a couple of different ways to gain access to the environment. If the device is personally owned and managed, the user can connect to the IBM Notes Traveler Server directly from the Personal Perimeter. If the device is intended to leverage the Work Perimeter, the device will connect to the Blackberry Enterprise Server (BES) 10 environment; the BES 10 server will act as a proxy for the device to access the IBM Notes Traveler environment.

It is intended that IBM Notes Traveler 9 will expand operating system support to include the IBM iSeries, Windows Server 12, Red Hat 6 (64-bit), and SUSE 11 (64-bit). Support for older versions of Red Hat and SUSE have been phased out, as the current version of the Domino Server will not support those operating systems. Please refer to the product documentation for further information and configuration assistance on the new platforms.

B

Mobile Device Management

The concept of deploying mobile communication devices in the corporate environment began with the introduction of the pager and has progressed from early **Personal Information Management (PIM)** devices, to cell phones, to smartphones, and now tablet devices. As more corporate and client data is communicated through and stored on mobile devices, corporate security and Information Technology (IT) departments have sought to protect corporate information. The development of solutions to secure corporate data has grown and these technologies have been labeled **Mobile Device Management (MDM)** solutions.

The goal of MDM solutions is to secure not only the devices through controlling features such as cameras, GPS, and other functionalities, but also the ability to manage corporate data on the phone. It is important to understand the differences between corporate and personal data when deploying an MDM solution. Many corporate IT and legal departments are concerned about protecting sensitive data; this is often too narrow of a label as some contents within an e-mail or contact data may not contain sensitive data, but are protected because they fall within the corporate mail container.

The requirements and ultimate selection and use of a Mobile Device Management (MDM) product depends on the overall security requirements in the environment and what other functions are trying to be addressed through the implementation of the solution, such as device tracking or asset control. Prior to implementing an additional layer of complexity and potentially expense, it is important to understand the solutions that are available within the environment (such as IBM Notes Traveler or Microsoft Exchange Active Sync) and how they can be leveraged to deploy an effective solution.

Types of devices in the environment

In the past, typically mobile devices were thought of as cell phones (or pagers) that had the ability for two-way communication. Securing simple communication devices was simple and was provided by the company that provided the technology, such as a cellular communication company. The company provided the technology and could control and secure the use of the device. With the expansion of corporate communications to include heavier reliance on electronic messaging to communicate internally and externally within the corporate environment, the expansion of evolution of technology such as Microsoft's ActiveSync technology and RIM's Blackberry Devices and Communication protocol made leveraging smartphone technology viable in a corporate setting.

The management and control of the devices were effective and efficient; the corporation typically owned the device, service, and delivery mechanism. Corporate IT security policies were typically built upon the level of security that could be provided through the mobile technology (or variances were granted) to ensure the ability to leverage the expanding technology within the environment. As the elements of the corporate communication devices expanded into the consumer market, vendors such as Microsoft and Google began developing and deploying solutions that mimicked the corporate solutions with consumer focus.

Consumer-focused devices

Consumer-focused devices such as the iPhone and Android-based smartphones were introduced into the corporate environment. There is great debate concerning the number of mobile devices currently being used globally, but it is clear that the growth of the use in this type of technology is far outpacing personal computers and eventually will exceed all other types of technology purchased and used.

These devices are being used for not only personal communications, but also for corporate communications as well. IT departments began purchasing devices and communication solutions to meet the demand of the end user community. Eventually, this led to many companies adopting a new strategy for mobile devices, Bring Your Own Device (BYOD). The BYOD strategy allows end users to procure and manage the technology that they choose to leverage for communication, and the corporation and IT department does not have to manage to a consumer-driven focus. Ultimately, the concept of BYOD has expanded for many companies to include tablets, personal computers, smart car communication systems, and eventually televisions.

The shift to BYOD has been popular with end users and some elements of the corporate structure, but it does bring more complications such as management of devices, information contained on the devices, and ultimately, the method of communicating with the device. The use of MDM within the environment allows for the management across devices and platforms to effectively secure corporate information. The protection and management of the end users' personal data may ultimately be assisted with the use of an MDM solution, but should not be the focus.

Mobile information

Mobile communications devices are leveraged for a wide variety of reasons, namely corporate and personal. As a result, it is easy to have different functions merge or connect through the use of end users. The following diagram outlines the different types of users for mobile devices:

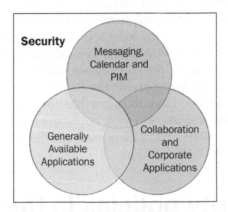

Messaging, calendar, and personal information management

This information is typically corporate in nature and is contained within the corporate communication tools. All information is synchronized with the device through a secondary source like an IBM Domino or Microsoft Exchange Server through a tool such as IBM Traveler or a proprietary service like Good Technology or Blackberry Enterprise Server. The security and information protection is handled by the tool managing the information in the environment.

Collaboration and corporate applications

As mobile technology has evolved in the corporate infrastructure, tools and resources have evolved to allow for the corporate environment to extend to mobile devices. Tools such as File repositories and Instant Messaging can be extended to allow mobile users to communicate and leverage the corporate collaborative environment. This data is typically managed by the tool that is delivering the resources to the device or through tools that exist on the device; the management of these tools can effectively be accomplished through the use of an MDM solution.

Generally available applications

Consumer-based applications that provide corporate type functionality are available through consumer sites such as the Google and Apple App stores. These popular applications, such as Dropbox, are tools that allow for the storage and synchronization of files across many platforms. Some corporate environments want to limit the use of external applications to minimize the federation spread of corporate information outside the controlled corporate environment. Typical consumer-focused applications are provided by the vendor and do not meet the standards typically found in corporate security policies to protect data from leaving the corporate environment and being housed outside in an uncontrolled environment. The corporation may purchase a service and provide it to the end users to meet requirements; these solutions will have more corporate controls in place. The management and "lock down" of this type of utility will likely require an MDM solution.

Mobile security policies in the environment

It is important to determine the security policies that need to be put in place within the mobile environment and how it compares to other policies within the overall corporate architecture. The current mobile space is different from traditional IT implementations or those through proprietary vendors who tightly control all aspects of the security. It is very difficult to leverage current security policies as outlined and extend them to a mobile environment. It is critical to identify the needs of the environment and what components of the security policy can and should be met, given the device ownership and uses. Corporate information needs to be secured, but limiting the use of a device, whether it is the internal GPS or camera, needs to be managed appropriately to ensure all applications function properly for all uses of the device. The mobile security industry typically identifies data, communication, and device security as the three main topics that need to be handled in a security policy.

Corporate data and information

Some of the data that is stored on the device whether at rest or in transit needs to be secured; the broader question though is what data sets need to be covered. Personal data belonging to the owner of the device may be sensitive to the owner, but is not important or deemed to be corporate data and therefore, should be left out of the policy. Corporate data such as business contact information, electronic messages, documents, and corporate applications need to have their contents secured against theft of data. Defining what can and cannot be stored on the device and how to effectively secure the data while on the device or if stolen should be clearly identified. Each organization will need to determine the types of data that need to be secured, and the importance assigned to each data set.

Network/communications

The communication of information has to be secure. Typically, corporate IT departments will have IT security standards in place that govern the use of secondary authentication and where communication devices can be placed in the network. It is important to understand that this needs to extend to the ability for end users to leverage Wi-Fi resources (secured and unsecured) along with differing communication companies. Securing the transit of the data is important; therefore, leveraging HTTPs over HTTP and VPN technology over secure data networks will be important to articulate.

Devices

By definition, mobile devices are intended to move with the user of the device. This creates a situation where human error or malicious behavior can compromise the device and ultimately, the data and communication that the devices leverage. The ability to locate, identify, and ultimately manage the device remotely is important. The security policy should deal with the human factors of security, such as loaning the device or leaving it unattended in a public space, but also with the loss of control that comes from the human failures. The process for identifying data and resources to be removed and the ability to manage the removal of data and service is vital for an effective mobile security policy.

Legal requirements and government regulations

There are a number of regulated industries that leverage mobile communication; it is important to understand the impacts of government regulations before completing a security policy. Government regulations such as the **Health Insurance Portability and Accountability Act (HIPAA)** require the protection of personal sensitive data. It is important to understand how all prevailing laws and regulations affect the mobile environment and potential security requirements.

Determining the types of devices that will be supported

The next step is to determine what devices will be supported based on who owns the device and the service being provided. As noted earlier, the introduction of non-corporate owned assets through a BYOD program can add complexity to the device and service that is required. The ownership and maintenance of devices will significantly impact the policy and how it is developed. This is important because in many cases the device may be owned by the end user, but the service is being provided by the corporate environment. As noted earlier, when people think of devices, the first product many think of is a smartphone, but there are many other devices that exist in the world today that significantly impact the delivery of technology to end users; when looking at Apple technology as an example, the iPhone, iPad, and iPod must all be considered due to how they leverage different operating systems.

Although it seems strange to consider for some people, smart television usage is growing with the inclusion of Wi-Fi, Internet-based applications, and cameras. These sorts of smart televisions can connect to the corporate environment and allow for the hosting of a web conference through the corporate infrastructure. The management of these devices and the ability for end users to leverage them in the corporate environment need to be identified with the appropriate policies put in place.

Determine if a pure MDM solution is required in the environment

It is important to understand what is being gained through the deployment of an MDM solution over the native features that are present in the devices and the current infrastructure. These technologies offer the utilization of standard features that are delivered within the products such as the IBM Traveler service or Microsoft Exchange natively. It is also important to understand if the solution that is being considered can be leveraged within the environment for other elements of the technology infrastructure; adding another component that could be covered by another current infrastructure adds complexity and can potentially add little value.

Tools such as IBM Endpoint Manager and Microsoft System Manager can offer a robust environment that spans the complete IT environment within the corporation, if it is determined that an MDM solution is required to meet security standards. Broader MDM solutions will collect data on environment usage and should manage a complete inventory of devices and services being utilized within the architecture. If an MDM solution is identified as required, it is important to ensure that tools such as this should be leveraged rather than multiple point solutions that do not meet the security requirements of the environment.

Elements of device management

The following sections will review the aspects of traditional MDM solutions in the marketplace (this is not intended to be an exhaustive list or a comparison of solutions). These solutions will not only increase security within your environment, but they will also add complexity and costs.

The following gives a broad overview of the different elements of MDM that exist within product offerings on the market today. A lot of this technology is an outcropping of the technology that was delivered with the Blackberry Enterprise Server.

Specific management of the device

Managing the device and controlling it through an inventory process is key to understanding what exists in the environment and what assets are required to be supported. The specific management of the device as an asset is typically accomplished through the following functions:

- **Inventory management**: This determines the devices in the environment and identifying ownership of the asset. This allows for management of the physical asset as a part of the corporate IT asset management process.

- **Use of VPN, Wi-Fi, cellular, and so on**: These perform managing the types of access that devices have to the network, whether the device is accessing the environment through cellular or Wi-Fi (secure or unsecure) technology will impact the protection afforded the environment.

- **Updates and compliance**: As new operating systems, applications, and policies are identified and deployed, it is important that the devices are maintained and do not stay in a static state. The MDM solution should be able to manage the compatibility and update process to ensure required software along with software and security policy updates are deployed.

Leveraging MDM for application management

Managing the applications on the device to ensure that all required applications exist, and those applications that could compromise corporate data are not installed or allowed cross-application access on the device.

- **A review of installed applications**: This compiles a list of applications installed on the devices. This can be invasive if the device is part of a BYOD strategy, but understanding exposure is a key first step.

- **Distributing and managing corporate applications**: These identify applications that are required on the device such as corporate VPN or security software that is required to ensure proper security on the device, or determine which applications should not be present as they represent a risk to corporate security.

- **Recommended applications**: These provide the recommended applications that exist within the app stores, such as editors, specific mapping, or GPS tools.

Management of data on the device

The data that exists on the device can be split into two easy categories: corporate and personal. No matter who the owner of the device or the provider of the connectivity services is, both types of data will exist on the device. It is important to understand how to manage both types of data; the removal of data should be selective, while the protection of the data should be universal. The entire device can be compromised through theft or loss; therefore, partial and complete wipe capabilities along with proper encryption and security need to exist.

- **Selective wipe**: This refers to removing only specific data that is relevant to the corporation, such as e-mail, calendar, and PIM data, ensuring that personal data to the device owner remains or is controlled by the owner is important. This includes specific applications and should not be limited to collaboration tools that exist on the device from one provider.

- **Complete wipe**: There are instances when a complete device needs to be wiped and all data should be removed. Some data, such as that located in programs like Dropbox, needs to be removed from the device even though the application is not a corporate app.

- **Remote lock**: Some devices that are stolen or accidently lost need to be locked down to avoid the loss of corporate data. The ability to lock the device remotely is a key requirement when dealing with mobile security.

- **Password and encryption**: The requirement of device-level password policies and the employment of encryption policies needs to be enforced on the devices to minimize security risks.

- **Lockdown of select applications**: If the security policy is set that devices attached to the corporate environment cannot leverage resources such as the camera or specific applications such as YouTube, Facebook, and so on, the solution should support the enforcement of internal policies.

- **Location of data**: With the extensibility of the corporate environment to the Cloud through readily available consumer services, there is a potential of mixing personal and corporate data in consumer containers in the Cloud. If limiting exposure of corporate data to the Cloud is within the security policy, it is important to identify known services and manage access.

Access control

Controlling access to the environment by certain devices, operating systems, or certificate credentials should be managed. Some devices and recently released operating systems may cause problems within the corporate environment due to incompatibilities. Additionally, if the end user mistakenly or intentionally stops communicating back to corporate resources, it is important to identify these issues and correct the situation to avoid complaints and issues.

- **Synchronization**: It is important that the device communicates with the corporate infrastructure and mail/calendar/PIM information along security processes which are extended to the devices. If this is not managed properly, the device will get out of sync and cause issues.

- **Password/certificate management**: The management of different passwords and certificates is important for the ease of the device usage, but can cause exposures to the corporate environment. The management of issuing, controlling, and removing security credentials is vital.

- **Device type/OS management**: The ability to restrict and manage the device based on the device type and operating system will greatly determine the level by which you upgrade and manage the corporate environment.

Potential solutions

There are a number of strong MDM solutions on the market with each providing different advantages and disadvantages. MDM products and features change as the market environment changes, which is rapidly. It is important to identify changes that impact your environment and address changes within your deployed environment against the vendors providing the services. It is important to work with each provider to ensure compliance. This appendix is intended to provide an overview of the process; please conduct a complete security and device review prior to deploying the solution that best meets the corporate requirements.

A strong starting point to understand the current players in the market is the Gartner Magic Quadrant for Mobile Device Management Software (subscription to Gartner or purchase of the individual report may be required). While one analyst's view of a large and diverse marketplace should not be viewed as complete, the Magic Quadrant information does provide a strong foundation of the market, players, and information about solutions provided.

Summary

The management of mobile access to the environment is extremely complex and requires a thorough understanding of the corporate goals for mobile communication and security requirements in the environment. The expansion of differing types of mobile devices has allowed for more flexibility by the end users and management to meet the needs of the organization. It is important to ensure that the corporate environment is not compromised in delivering the resources to the end users.

Additionally, devices and data contained on them become assets of the corporate environment when they attach to the environment; therefore, the concept of BYOD or corporate-owned assets gets fuzzy once corporate data resides on the device. Deploy the right solution for the environment and the end users, while securing the corporate data and protecting the broader environment.

C

Tips to Help You Protect Your Mobile Device

The United States **Federal Bureau of Investigation (FBI)** and the **National White Collar Crime Center (NW3C)** established a unit called the **Internet Crime Complaint Center (IC3)** to provide a single point of contact for people reporting Internet-related criminal complaints. After researching the complaints, the IC3 refers them to the appropriate law enforcement or regulatory agency. The IC3 also publishes warnings on new threats to people via technology. The unit developed a list of tips to help you protect your mobile device, available at `http://www.fbi.gov/scams-safety/e-scams`, and copied here in its entirety (as of July 9, 2013).

- When purchasing a smartphone, know the features of the device, including the default settings. Turn-off features of the device not needed, to minimize the attack surface of the device.

- Depending on the type of phone, the operating system may have encryption available. This can be used to protect the user's personal data in the case of loss or theft.

- With the growth of the application market for mobile devices, users should look at the reviews of the developer/company who published the application.

- Review and understand the permissions you are giving when you download applications.

- Passcode-protect your mobile device. This is the first layer of physical security to protect the contents of the device. In conjunction with the passcode, enable the screen lock feature after a few minutes of inactivity.

- Obtain malware protection for your mobile device. Look for applications that specialize in antivirus or file integrity that helps protect your device from rogue applications and malware.

- Be aware of applications that enable geo-location. The application will track the user's location anywhere. This application can be used for marketing but can also be used by malicious actors, raising concerns of assisting a possible stalker and/or burglaries.

- Jailbreaking or rooting is used to remove certain restrictions imposed by the device manufacturer or cell phone carrier. This allows the user nearly unregulated control over what programs can be installed and how the device can be used. However, this procedure often involves exploiting significant security vulnerabilities and increases the attack surface of the device. Anytime an application or service runs in "unrestricted" or "system" level within an operation system, it allows any compromise to take full control of the device.

- Do not allow your device to connect to unknown wireless networks. These networks could be rogue access points that capture information passed between your device and a legitimate server.

- If you decide to sell your device or trade it in, make sure you wipe the device (reset it to factory default) to avoid leaving personal data on the device.

- Smartphones require updates to run applications and firmware. If users neglect this, it increases the risk of having their device hacked or compromised.

- Avoid clicking on or otherwise downloading software or links from unknown sources.

- Use the same precautions on your mobile phone as you would on your computer when using the Internet.

D
Mobile Acceptable Use Policy Template

This appendix shows an example template that can be used by a company to create an Acceptable Use Policy for mobile devices. A company can have several types of these documents. The examples include:

- Acceptable use policy
- Privacy policy
- Conduct business guidelines
- Corporate social sharing policies

The appendix only shows an example for a mobile device acceptable use policy. You can have a single document that shows corporate owned document and one for BYOD. Another option is to have a combination of both policies into a single document that shows both. Keep in mind this is a sample template for your corporation to use. Your company will need to review local and/or government laws and determine what privacy issues that need to be addressed.

Mobile device acceptable use policy

A **Mobile Acceptable Use Policy** (**MAUP**) is a formal agreement between an organization and the employees from that organization. This document sets out the acceptable rules for mobile device usage. Also this document will review any penalties that could be applied resulting from the rule violation from incorrect use of mobile devices.

Overview

The purpose of this policy is to define procedures, standards, and corporate impacts for end users that use a mobile device for access to corporate data. This device policy applies to, but is not limited to, any device that is used for corporate access. The device types, noted in this section, primarily are focused on Bring Your Own Device (BYOD) to work, but also can impact any mobile device provided by the company. These devices can include:

- Smartphone (of any type)
- Mobile phones
- Any style of tablet computers
- PCs
- Notebook or Laptop (or any device that has access to the corporate network)
- Portable media devices, netbooks, or PDAs

Policy applicability

This policy was created to protect corporate data and the corporation's reputation. It is imperative that each person manages their mobile devices to make sure that the corporate network and data is safe and secure. Every employee must sign this agreement and must follow all the corporate rules. This policy will apply to all employees, contractors, vendors, and/or anyone that will connect to the corporate network.

Rules

The following example rules can be used in your BYOD template. Each rule must be evaluated to make sure it fits your corporate environment:

- These rules include BYOD devices that all must be registered with the corporate **Mobile Device Management (MDM)** system or manager. This is an automated process and must be completed by all users. Before a device can be connected to the corporate network, the employee must obtain an approval from their manager. Management can terminate a device connection at any time for any reason.
- The corporation may install virus and/or protection software on this device any time. End users must accept the corporate network software or they will lose access to the network.
- Access and use of the device that connects to the corporate network will be tracked as needed by the corporation.

- If a device is deemed "compromised" then it will be blocked from accessing the corporate network.

- The end user will be responsible for notifying the company if a device is stolen within one business day.

- If the device is lost and/or stolen then all the data, personal and business, will be wiped from the device if the device goes online and the device will be blocked from accessing the corporate network.

- Since this is a BYOD device, the owner is responsible for replacing the physical device if the device is lost, stolen, or damaged.

- The company will enforce security on the device and will force a password change down to each device that will expire every 90 days. Passwords are never shared with anyone at any time.

- The end user will not jailbreak devices or execute any rooting on the Android devices.

- Data that is hosted on the mobile device (for example, corporate applications or e-mail) is never transferred or copied to a non-approved corporate application. Refer to `https://corporate.mobile.example.com` for more information.

- Sharing corporate data on any non-corporate site (for example, shared social sites) is a violation of the company policies and is grounds for termination.

- The user will keep the software on the mobile devices up-to-date with the latest version.

- The user will only install apps from trusted locations.

- It will be the end user's responsibility to make sure that people are not shoulder reading their material. In some cases, a glare screen can be purchased that can help with this issue.

Disciplinary action

Violating the corporate policy or any of its specific rules will result in specific disciplinary action. This action can include termination and can include notification of local and/or federal authorities under local, state, and/or federal laws.

Company owned devices

A Mobile Acceptable Use Policy (MAUP) is a formal agreement between an organization and the employees from that organization. This document sets out the acceptable rules for mobile device usage. Also, this document will review any penalties that could be applied resulting from the rule violation from incorrect use of mobile devices.

Overview

This specific policy will focus primarily on devices that are provided to the employee by the corporation. These devices can include:

- Smartphone (of any type)
- Mobile Phones
- Any style of table computers
- PCs
- Notebook or Laptop

Rules for corporate devices

All corporate devices must be registered with the corporate Mobile Device Management (MDM) system. This is an automated process and must be completed by all users.

Before a device can be connected to the corporate network, the employee must obtain an approval from their manager.

Rules

The following example rules can be used when a corporate device is provided to you by the end user. Each rule must be evaluated to make sure it fits your corporate environment:

- Management can terminate a device connection any time, for any reason, to the corporate network.
- The corporation will install virus and/or protection software on corporate owned phone/devices. End users must accept corporate network software or they will lose access to the device and the corporate network.
- Access and use of the device will be tracked as needed by the corporation.
- If a device is deemed "compromised", then it will be blocked from accessing the corporate network. (This can happen without notification to the end user)
- The end user will be responsible for notifying the company if a device is stolen within one business day. All the data will be wiped from the device if the device goes online, and the device will be blocked from accessing the corporate network.
- If the device is lost and/or stolen then all the data, personal and business, will be wiped from the device if the device goes online, and the device will be blocked from accessing the corporate network.

- Since this device is a corporate device, end users may not use the device for personal use.

- The end users may only use the corporate provided device for business use only. The device may not be used to run a personal business and/or for any personal use.

- Since this is a corporate owned device, the corporation is responsible for device support, maintenance, and if the device is lost or damaged.

- The company will enforce security on the device and will force a password change down to each device that will expire every 90 days. Passwords are never shared with anyone anytime.

- The end user will not jailbreak the device or execute any rooting on the Android devices.

- The user will keep the software on the mobile devices up-to-date with the latest version.

- The user will only install apps from trusted locations.

- It will be the end user's responsibility to make sure that people are not shoulder reading their material. In some cases, a glare screen can be purchased that can help with this issue.

- Data that is hosted on the mobile device (for example, corporate applications or e-mail) is never transferred or copied to a non-approved corporate application. Refer to `https://corporate.mobile.example.com` for more information.

- Sharing corporate data on any non-corporate site (for example, shared social sites) is a violation of the company policies and are grounds for termination.

- The owner will not execute any illegal actions on the device.

Disciplinary action

Violating the corporate policy or any of its specific rules can result in specific disciplinary action. This action can include termination of employment and can include notification of the appropriate authorities under local, state, and/or federal laws.

Glossary

BYOD: This is a term that describes the users that will bring their own mobile device/tablet to the workplace. This is the inverse to where a company will purchase a device and provide it directly to the employees for business use on the corporate computing environment.

Jailbreak/Rooting: Jailbreaking a mobile device (phone/tablets) is a method of removing the software limitations that mobile device companies will place on specific devices. These limits normally are a part of an overall security method and should not be removed. Device Jailbreaking is never allowed by the company.

MDM: This stands for Mobile Device Management. The company uses the MDM software to help protect the security of the device as well as the security of the corporate software and data.

Corporate Owned Device: This is the inverse of a BYOD device. The corporation will own the device and provide it to the end user/employee (in some cases a vendor) for use during the time of employment and/or a specific project. The device must be returned to the company if the employee is terminated and/or the end of the specific project.

Procedure to enable a device for corporate access

To enable a device for corporate access, complete the following steps:

1. Read the Mobile Device Acceptable Use Policy (present in this document).
2. Sign and date in the spaces following this section.
3. Return a copy of this signed document to the mobile device manager or your manager. Be sure you can print your name in the spaces following this section.

Your signature provides agreement to the following terms of this document/policy:

- I have read and received a copy of the Mobile Device Acceptable Policy (present in this document).
- I will only use the device for business requirements only (Company owned only).
- I understand and agree that mobile devices will not be connected to corporate systems, computers, or networks without proper approvals.
- If the device is employee-owned, then I understand and agree that the security and replacement of a device becomes my responsibility. If the device is corporate-owned, then the employee will work with the help desk to determine next steps and/or replacement processes. Also, the employee will call the help desk anytime the device may be compromised.

- I understand and agree that any violation of this policy can result in termination of my employment and civil or criminal penalties.
- I understand that the device can be removed from the corporate mobile system anytime.

_____

Employee name

_____

Employee signature

_____

Employee title

_____

Date

E

The History of Social Networking, the Internet, and Smartphones

Not so many years ago, when a new college student drove off to college for the first time the parents asked, "Do you have enough change to use a payphone and call home in an emergency on your trip?" Today, this concept of carrying change for a payphone is largely a thing of the past; the vast majority of us carry cell phones. Payphones used to be on the side of every highway and in the parking lot of every gas station. Now, these payphones are becoming rare. It is just assumed that everyone has access to a cell phone. In fact, a lot of people do not even have land lines in their home. After all, why should you pay for two phones when you are always reachable on your cell phone?

Now, when your child sets off to college, you warn them, "Do not text while driving". The cell phone is not just an instrument for making phone calls. Texting has become a preferred use.

Texting allows the user to quickly communicate with another person without interrupting whatever they are doing. It is quiet and has even resulted in the creation of a new language. Instead of telling someone that their comment was funny, one might text **LOL (laughing out loud)**. Do you need to take a quick break? Just type **BRB (be right back)**. The list of acronyms can seem endless, and is changing at a breathtaking pace. Among some, these acronyms have even begun to leave the mobile space and enter our daily conversation, as commonly used words.

Another significant cultural force in recent decades has been the phenomenon of the so-called social networking sites. For example, if someone wants to keep up with you, the first thing they might ask is, "Are you on Facebook?" Families keep up on Facebook, sharing photos or videos of the baby's first steps. In fact, it has become rare for people to exchange phone numbers, because many would rather communicate online than by voice. With many modern smartphones, phone numbers have actually become relatively unnecessary, as you can simply click on the username or the Facebook ID of your friend, and then automatically get connected to them, through the account's associated phone number. Another primary advantage of social networking sites is that you can communicate on Facebook regardless of the time; no more worrying about waking your friend up in the middle of the night if you want to send them a quick message.

Another use that has become popular is to find people you may not have heard from in a long time. You can search Facebook and resume old friendships, and you can even rekindle old romances.

The Internet

In this world of Youtube, Facebook, Hulu, and Twitter, it may be hard to imagine that the Internet has only been an integral part of our society for some three decades. The Internet, as we know it today, was originally conceived in 1969 as a method by which colleges could share information and research. Two years later, in 1971, e-mail was born and the @ symbol was first used to separate the name of the user from the service provider. Later in the decade, the PC modem was introduced to facilitate transatlantic communication, and shortly thereafter the bulletin board was developed as a method of easily sharing messages on the network. In 1978, the first spam, unsolicited commercial e-mail, message was sent. One might say that, with spam's introduction, the essential elements of our modern technology culture were firmly in place.

 For more information check out, http://www.zakon.org/robert/internet/timeline/ and http://www.internetsociety.org/internet/what-internet/history-internet/brief-history-internet.

The explosion of the World Wide Web continued throughout the 1980s and into the 90s with CompuServe and AOL as early adopters. The web was formalized in 1994 when Tim Berners-Lee created the **URL (Uniform Resource Locator)**. The significance of this innovation cannot be underestimated; it provided a reliable method for locating and accessing information on the Internet by organizing online data into addresses. This URL format made accessing the web data easier for humans to read. The notation of this method is familiar to most of us today, `http://` followed by some site-specific title, which was then followed by `.com`, `.org`, or a number of other specifiers, also known as top-level domains. This innovation rendered the Internet truly accessible; to find information online, all you needed was the ability to type out a URL. You did not need to understand how to code or how to modify HTML.

Of course, the most significant development for most of us was the introduction, as early as 1990, of the search engine. Which search engine was first is still a matter of debate; some argue that the search tool Archie, developed by researchers at McGill University, was the first with the ability of finding files. Others argue that Gopher, a tool developed by students at the University of Minnesota, was the first true search engine. Regardless of which was first, the search engine quickly became one of the most vital innovations that rendered the resources of the Internet accessible to the general population. By the time Google was introduced in 1997, a number of other search engines, from Yahoo! to Altavista, had already been utilized by millions of people around the world. With a search engine, you didn't even need to enter a URL; you could just type the word you were interested in learning about, and a list of results would be displayed for your perusal.

Today, we can access the Internet from our laptop, our tablet, our cell phone, and even from certain appliances such as refrigerators and televisions. The Internet is an integral aspect of practically every part of our lives. With wireless Internet and telecommunications networks, the Internet can be accessed anywhere. Coffee shops, such as Starbucks and hotels, advertise the availability of wireless connections. Now, you can work, chat with friends, go on Facebook, blog, or play a game practically anywhere. Even resumes, which previously were done exclusively on paper, are compiled electronically on word processor applications and then e-mailed to potential employers online. Want to search for job openings? Go online and browse from a seemingly countless variety of job websites, from Monster to `Indeed.com`. This goes both ways, of course. Just as you can search for employers, employers can search for you on professional networking sites, such as LinkedIn. In 2012, it's hard to imagine that, only some three decades ago, job seekers had to peruse the paper for openings and students had to visit the library to do research for school projects.

Social networking

Facebook was not the first social networking site. It wasn't even the first to provide a network of friends or a "wall", where friends could post messages, images, and links. Social networking, or the concept of using the Internet to form relationships and keep in touch with friends, may have begun as early as the mid 90s when sites such as Classmates.com and Geocities first gained prominence. Classmates.com, which is still operating today, was a social networking site that attempted to locate people based on publicly available information such as high school graduation classes or school enrollment databases. The idea was that, if you wanted to reconnect with an old high school flame, you could do just that with Classmates.com.

Sites such as Geocities and Tripod alternately offered the advantages of an online network of contacts. On these sites, a user would sign up for an account, and then begin to create their own online presence in the form of a dedicated website. The social networking aspect of these sites was manifested by the list of contacts or friends, which allowed members of these services to connect with one another, send messages, and link to each other's personal websites.

The first site to synthesize these two approaches to social networking was Friendster, which launched in the year 2002. Friendster developed the concept of degrees of social networks. Friendster attempted to connect its members with new contacts based upon how close they were with a member's other friends. For example, if you were friends with Jacob and Bill, and both of them were friends with Jane, then Friendster might attempt to connect you with Jane. This was a novel approach to social networking, because it allowed for an intuitive manner for building social networks in an online space. After all, just because a person hasn't personally connected with someone online, does not mean that they do not know them or that they would not like to connect with them. In effect, Friendster made it easier to interact with and find people they might already know.

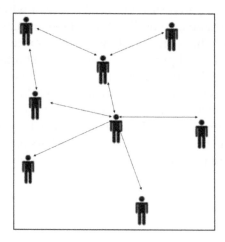

Similar to Friendster, Myspace launched in the year 2003. This service's primary advantage was its introduction of a message-board style format to a member's homepage. By creating a "myspace", a member could organize a space in which their friends and contacts could leave comments. One way of thinking of this development may be by thinking of guestbooks which predated and inspired it; on a guestbook, a visitor could leave a comment about the site or the site's author. This comment would remain indefinitely for public viewing unless the site's author chose to delete it. The difference in Myspace was only that a member's entire site may be regarded as an elaborate and personalized guestbook. On Myspace, a member could adorn the top of their page with personal photos or even playable songs and videos. They could provide separate boxes that contained personal information, such as location, age, and marital status. While it was popular, Myspace was a primary destination within popular music, as most popular rock bands used the site in lieu of a permanent web address; they used it to announce things such as concert dates and C.D. release parties.

In 2003, LinkedIn introduced an entirely different approach to social networking. This site may be considered as a natural evolution of the social networking phenomenon; if many were already using social networking sites to connect with friends for informal purposes, why not use the same technology to allow employers and employees to find each other online? This is exactly the possibility that LinkedIn provided. On LinkedIn, an employer or employee could create an account, and populate that account with information about their qualifications or hiring requirements. Then, just as Friendster provided a search engine which allowed people to connect based on a matching profile criteria, LinkedIn would assist its members in matching qualifications with hiring needs. At its most basic level, LinkedIn was a professional database that allowed employers and employees to search for each other. What elevated this service, however, was the ability members had to then contact each other within LinkedIn's infrastructure; they didn't have to call each other if they didn't want to. They could just send a message online. As an additional benefit of this service, colleagues could create professional networks of friends within this formal networking context. LinkedIn was, for all intents and purposes, the professional version of social networking sites, such as Friendster.

In 2004, the most successful social networking site to date was first introduced; Facebook. Many of us already know the story of Facebook and its founder, Mark Zuckerberg. We may have learned about it from seeing the award-winning film, *The Social Network*, or we may have picked up some of the details from countless articles written about the staggering success of one of the world's most wealthy individuals. Facebook originally began as a social networking site exclusive to Harvard students. One might think of it as an upgraded and advanced version of Classmates.com; with Facebook, members could easily find Harvard students by searching for classmates based on coursework. For example, if you were enrolled in the fall to take Psychology 101, you could search the roll of other students and if they had accounts, peruse their Facebook profiles. If you so choose, you could then leave them a message that said you were excited to be taking a class with them. Facebook's success at Harvard quickly led to its expansion to many other universities. For the first several years of Facebook's existence, in fact, the service was exclusive to universities. It was only in 2006 that Facebook was first made available to the general public.

Mobiles

The dream of a phone you could use anywhere may be as old as the telephone itself. Before cell phones, the only way to make a phone mobile was to install one in a car; many may remember that the car-phone was one of the more famous status symbols of the 1980s.

This changed when, in 1983, Motorola released the first commercially available cell phone, called DynaTAC. Its asking price was a meager $ 3,995, and it boasted a whopping 30 minutes of talktime for the would-be trendsetters. While it was not able to text or surf the Internet, it did include an LED screen that allowed a user to recall and redial previously used phone numbers. Unfortunately, it was also the roughly the size and shape of a brick.

While the paltry feature set and high price point of the DynaTAC may seem ridiculous to those of us living in the 21st century, consumer demand for the product back in the 1980s was quite robust. In fact, the DynaTAC sold well enough for Motorola to introduce numerous iterations, with the last being released in the year 1993. It even made an impact on 1980s popular culture when Michael Douglas's character in the era-defining film *Wall Street* used one. The DynaTAC's allure is understandable when we consider that the device was, after all, the first commercially released phone which was not permanently tethered to a residence or vehicle. It was the first truly mobile phone.

This first device paved the way for models produced by competitors that boasted longer battery life and a more accessible price point. Cell phones were such a successful product, in fact, that by the 1990s it seemed as though everyone had one. What once had been a status symbol of the excessively wealthy had, by the 90s, become a common commodity which could be had for free if you just signed a multi-year contract.

The next step was taken in 1993 when the first cell phone to include features such as an organizer and fax machine was released. Produced by IBM under the name Simon, this phone was the world's first smartphone. Though large by today's standards, it possessed functions well beyond simply making phone calls, and thus foreshadowed the development of cell phones into one of the most essential devices of the 21st century.

On regular cell phones, you may not be able to fax your documents or manage your calendar, and you most certainly will not be able to download Apps, such as Whatsapp or Angry Birds, through an online application store (App Store). The main reason for this is that regular cell phones, which include popular models such as Motorola's Razr, are designed primarily to make phone calls; the few additional functions supported by these regular cell phones are generally not as extensive as those present in smartphones. In other words, regular cell phones are just that, regular phones.

Smartphones come in a wide variety of shapes, sizes, brands, and models. Some, like the Apple iPhone, Sony, Nokia, and Samsung Galaxy S, feature multi-touch screens that can display videos and pictures in high resolution. Others, such as particular models of Research in Motion's Blackberry line, possess a full keyboard as a built-in attachment but do not possess a touch screen. Regardless of the particular differences in each model, all of these phones are similar, in that they are designed to do far more than simply make phone calls. You might say that this is what makes them smart; their focus on their additional functions as opposed to their ability to serve as mobile telephones.

Released in 2007, the iPhone was originally conceived as an iPod with the added functionality of a cell phone. The original iPhone could make and receive phone calls, but it could also play music and interact online using Apple's Safari application, and it could surf the Internet. One of the more significant features of the iPhone was its multi-touch screen, which allowed a user to manipulate icons and folders without the need for attached buttons. On top of all of this, the iPhone sported a 2 megapixel digital camera and included an application store (App Store).

This robust feature set, combined with Apple's by then already established reputation as a technology trendsetter, resulted in the iPhone's unmitigated success upon its 2007 release. In fact, even before the device was released to the public, Apple's competitors were in the first stages of designing their own cell phones which would sport a similar set of features (`http://ign.com/articles/2010.06/24/ the-history-of-the-iphone`).

Upon its original release, the iPhone was most notable for the staggering array of tasks it could perform. A user could take a photo of a place they had visited, and then send this photo as an e-mail attachment to their friend. The user could then log onto Facebook or, at the time, MySpace through the Safari web browser and share comments on this or other photos with their friends. If the user wished, they could then download a game from the App Store and play for several minutes before deciding to text their friend on the included texting application. Most significantly, all of this could be done on the same device while the user rode the bus into town. The iPhone was a truly multi-functional device, which eliminated the need for other devices to perform the same number of tasks. Truly, the iPhone could do it all.

Subsequent iterations of the iPhone only cemented the success of the first release. In July 2008, Apple released the iPhone 3G. The primary feature of this device was in the title; it ran on the third generation of the mobile telecommunications network. The iPhone 3G was also the first generation of the device to include GPS functionality and an included maps application.

The iPhone 4S was released with some additional features in October, 2011. The primary feature of this release was the ability to save data to a cloud. The cloud functionality allowed a user to save data remotely, and to then access that data from either the same device or another device. This functionality also allowed a user to locate their phone geographically by utilizing a GPS tracking signal in the phone.

The difference between Android and iOS

Most of Apple's competitors use the Android mobile operating system to run their user interface. In fact, smartphones using the Android operating system composed 52 percent of the cell phone market share in the US as of October, 2012. (`http://www.engadget.com/2012/10/02/comscore-iphone-moved-up-to-34- percent-us-share-in-august/`).

Comparatively, the iPhone runs on iOS (**iPhone Operating System**). This is Apple's internally developed operating system, which cannot be used to operate other devices without Apple's permission (and Apple has not, as of the time of this writing, provided such permission to any other manufacturers). From the perspective of maintaining your mobile security, this is significant because Apple is the sole entity which is able to operate and monitor this platform. No other parties, large or small, may alter or edit this infrastructure and this results in a more secure environment for the end user.

The best way to understand the difference between the Android and the iOS operating systems for smartphones is by considering the difference between the Windows and Apple operating systems that run on PCs and Macintosh computers. Also keep in mind that Android is open source which encourages developers to make their own branch of the operating system. The iOS on iPhones only runs on Apple products like Android, runs on a variety of devices produced by a variety of manufactures.

The Android operating system, like the iOS on iPhone, is an operating system designed for use on smart devices with a multi-touch screen. The Android operating system is currently open source, which means that anyone can access the code and make alterations. What this means for the consumer is that the Android operating system can run quite differently on different phones that use it. Also applications designed for one formation of Android may not be supported on other Android devices.

As one might imagine, this lack of parity between Android phones can also create some problems for the end user in terms of performance and functionality. Some apps purchased on the Android App Store may only work on certain phones, and thus it is the user's responsibility to ensure that their phone can run the application in question before they choose to download it.

Let's not forget Windows

Windows 8, which was released shortly before the time of this writing, may represent the introduction of the third major player in the mobile space. Although Windows mobile has, until recently, been Microsoft's primary effort in the mobile space, the operating system has not been nearly as successful as iOS or Android. With the introduction of Windows 8, Microsoft appears to be positioning itself to compete with these two major mobile operating systems. The primary feature of Windows 8, as it pertains to mobile, is the introduction of the Windows Store. The new Windows Store will, according to Microsoft, allow various Microsoft devices to access applications that perform equitably on most of the company's devices. This will be accomplished through the use of Windows Live IDs, which Microsoft has already successfully implemented in Windows Live PC.

The following is a list of common devices, both iOS and Android, within the mobile space:

- Apple iPad (various generations)
- Apple iPhone (various generations)
- Apple iPod touch (various generations)
- Blackberry Torch 9800
- HTC Droid Incredible 2

- HTC Evo (various generations)
- HTC One X
- HTC Windows Phone 8X
- LG Lucid
- LG Intuition
- LG Optimus G
- Motorola Atrix HD
- Motorola Droid Razr
- Motorola Photon Q
- Nokia Lumia 920
- Samsung Galaxy Note II
- Samsung Galaxy Stratosphere
- Samsung Galaxy S III
- Nexus
- Samsung GALAXY S4
- Sony Xperia Z
- BlackBerry Z10 and Q10
- ZTE Grand S
- Huawei Ascend D2
- Asus Padfone
- Nokia Lumia 925

Text messaging, chatting, and video chatting

Throughout the 90s, the primary forms of online communication were e-mail, message boards, and newsgroups. As evidenced by the name, electronic mail (e-mail) was originally intended as an alternative to traditional mail. Those of us that remember e-mail in its earliest days may also remember how formal some of the first e-mails could be; users often imitated traditional mail format in every sense. Message boards and newsgroups were, however, a relatively informal method of online communication. Message boards and newsgroups were both advantageous because they allowed for topic-related threads, or conversation categories which could drive the focus of particular conversations. Additionally, of course, all of these forms of communication did not require an immediate response; unlike a phone conversation, a user could read a message and respond in their own time. The message, whether by e-mail or message board, would be posted regardless of whether the recipient was online or not.

To no small degree, these popular 90s technologies have influenced our mobile communications practices. Where, once, we might have posted a message to a friend on a message board or as a response to a newsgroup e-mail, today, many will simply send a text message as a part of their cell phone's **Short Message Service (SMS)**. The SMS service, though first developed in the late 1980s, did not enjoy widespread use among cell phone users until well into the mid-1990s. The format of these messages, like message board responses, is often informal and brief; text messages are only rarely intended as detailed conversations.

Another form of communication is known as **instant messaging (IM)**. Instant messaging is known as online chatting. IM provides real time exchange of messages, which is different from e-mail that in effect sends a batch of data. IM allows quick and efficient communication between people. This can be executed via one on one or even groups of users. Instant messaging is largely done through ICQ, Compuserve **AIM (Aol Instant Messenger)**, and IBM at the same time.

For more complex discussions, a modern mobile user might decide to use an application such as Whatsapp, so that they could send and receive responses in real time. Chatting came to prominence during the 90s with the advent of computer programs, such as ICQ, AIM, and **Microsoft Instant Messenger (MSN)**. These chat programs allowed a user the advantages of telephone conversations, in that they were real-time discussions, and a user would be aware when their conversant was connected or not through status notifications. Like with many previously computer-based activities, chatting has become increasingly popular as a mobile activity. Through applications such as WhatsApp, AIM, or MSN, a user can chat in real time with friends on their smartphones. Of course, this means that all of the risks inherent in chatting on computers have also been duplicated on the smartphone device.

A final method of mobile communication which is becoming increasingly popular is video chatting. This method may have no equivalent in the 1990s but, with the advent of programs such as Skype, has become an all too common method of talking and seeing our friends and family regardless of their physical location. Recent iterations of certain smartphones, in fact, even include a video chatting feature as a part of their integrated cell phone infrastructure; this means that there is no need to download a separate application if one wishes to video chat.

In our modern and mobile world, there seems to be no limit to the varieties of methods by which we can communicate and interact. We can video chat, text chat, send instant messages, comment on photos, send tweets, and of course, call someone.

Many small businesses have even begun to use smartphones and tablets as a method of collecting payment from their customers. For example, Amy's Ice Cream, an ice cream store located in Austin, Texas, uses an app called Pay Anywhere, to swipe customer credit cards and collect payment. This popular app is associated with a credit card add-on that, when attached to the charger port on a tablet or a smartphone allows the device to read the credit information for payment processing.

Because of the bewildering possibilities afforded by App Stores, smartphones are increasingly being utilized as a method of simplifying our most common financial transactions. Today, we can use our smartphones to check our account balance, transfer funds from one account to another, pay for parking, purchase products through various online outlets, and even take payment for goods on those occasions when we are the ones selling goods. Although there are still some limits to what our smartphones can do, we should expect that these limits will only continue to recede as the capabilities of these devices are further realized.

Index

D

damage coverage 136
data
  about 43, 173, 180
  corporate data 173, 180
  personal data 173, 180
data-at-rest 100
data encryption 99
data encryption, Android
  about 100
  drawbacks 100
data encryption, iOS 100
data-at-reset 100
data-in-transit 100
data-in-use 100
data location 83, 181
data management 180
data segregation 83
data theft 61, 74
data thieves 48
deceptive phishing 74
demilitarized zone. *See* DMZ
demographic information
  collecting 12
Developer Distribution Agreement 48
device
  accessing, through application
       downloads 106
  accessing, through attachment 106
  access control, within corporate
       environment 181
  data 180
  data management 180
  enabling, for corporate access 190
  testing 128
  types 174
  used, for corporate communication 174
  wiping 159
device hacks
  about 156
  addressing 157, 158
  checklist 160
  differentiating, with profile hacks 156
  indication 155
  post actions 157, 159, 162
  unawareness 155

device profile
  about 151, 152
  Android profile 153
  Apple profile 152, 153
device, types
  about 181
  consumer-focused devices 174
  determining 178
device, wiping
  decision making 159
  full wipe 160
  partial wipe 160
Digby 60
Digital Convergence Corporation 17
digital identity 42
digital information 42
Digital Rights Management. *See* DRM
direct connection
  configuring, to IBM Traveler Server 167
disaster recovery (DR) 84
disciplinary action 187, 189
DMZ 38
DNS-based phishing (pharming) 74
Domain Name System (DNS) 74
Domino Directory Assistance 166
Domino Server 163, 166
DoSomething.org 149
downloaded applications
  about 101
  antivirus software, on smartphones 101
DRM
  about 31
  URL, for info 31
DroidKungFu 84
Dropbox 80, 176
DWA 168
DynaTAC 198

E

Electronic Chip Identifier. (eCID) 90
electronic messaging 163
elements, MDM 179
e-mail 202
Encrypted Backup setting 93
encryption policies 181

J

J2ME 14
jailbreak 31
jailbreaking 94, 190
Jupiter Networks 47

K

Kaspersky 8
key 99
keyloggers attack 75
Kryptos 100

L

legitimate programs 9
licensing information, IBM Notes
        Traveler 171
lifetime warranty 130
LinkedIn 195, 197
location-based marketing, type
  check-in services 57
location-based services (LBS) 82
LOL (laughing out loud) 194
longer password
  creating 97, 98
Lookout Mobile Security
  example, of toll fraud 70
Loozfon 68
lost coverage 136
lost devices
  wiping 108

M

mail routing server 38
mail servers
  about 166
  location 166
malfunction
  addressing, to customer service
        representatives 127
  describing, to customer service
        representatives 128
  determining, for BYOD 158
  unresolved 129

malicious app, downloading
  precautions 102
malware
  about 44, 68, 69
  FakeInst 71
  FinFisher 69
  Loozfon 69
  mobile device, attacking 69
  SMS spoofing 71
  toll fraud 69
  used, for hacking smartphones 9
  used, for infecting smartphones 45
malware attacks
  unawareness 8
malware-based phishing 74
manufacturer
  about 122
  contacting, for hardware malfunction 123
manufacturer warranty 130
McAfee 101 7
MDM
  about 28, 38, 164, 173, 186, 190
  benefits 30
  elements 179
  features 30
  functions 179
  installing 28, 29, 30
  leveraging, for application
        management 180
  managing, corporate data on the phone 173
  used, for protecting frontend network 28
  used, for securing corporate data 175
MDM products 32
MDM solution
  about 179
  availability 182
  determining 179
MEID 90
message boards 202
messaging server 39
Microsoft 158, 163, 201
Microsoft 365 Apps 80
Microsoft ActiveSync technology 174
Microsoft Exchange Active Sync 173
Microsoft Exchange Server 175
Microsoft Instant Messenger (MSN) 203
Microsoft System Manager 179

profile hacks
about 156
differentiating, with device hacks 156
Pumpkin Maker 53

Q

QR boxes
reading 18
usage 18
QR code generator
URL 18
QR reader app 18
Quick Response Code (QR Code)
about 18
creating 18-20

R

Real Time Operating Systems (RTOS) 14
recommended applications 180
Red Hat 6 172
remote lock 181
restore, Apple device 153
restore, mobile device 153
retailers
customer location, tracking 57
reverse proxy 38, 166, 167
RIM Blackberry Devices 174
rooting 31, 94
Rovio 52

S

Safe Harbor Act 83
SafeSearch 147
Sale of Goods ACT 132
Salt Lake City 21
Samsung 158
URL, for online assistant 157
Samsung Galaxy S 199
Samsung Galaxy S3 158
screenloggers attack 75
search engine 195
search engine phishing 75
security 82
security compliance 83
security policy 181

security settings
creating 170
security threats 68
selective wipe 180
Service Level Agreement. *See* SLA
service providers 122
session cookie 43
sexting 146, 147
sexually explicit text message (sext) 146
Short Message Service (SMS) 53, 165, 203
SIM
about 89
used, for identifying mobile device 89
SIM card 89
Simple tether configuration tool 36
Skulls 84
Skype 203
SLA 120, 121
SlideShare 80
SmartMan
URL 32
smartphone activities
tracking 12
smartphone revolution
precursors 10
smartphones
about 7
accessing, through SMS messaging
attacks 106
categories 134
cloud computing, designing for data
retrieval 21
features 14
hacking, malware used 9
hacking, viruses used 9
hardware issue 123
infecting, malware used 45
maintaining 133
operating system error 124
operating systems 14
personal computers, comparing to 44
preventative measures, for hacking 92, 94
protecting, from hackers 92
reach out 46
replacing 133
revolutionizing 13
risks 7, 8

Trojan
   smartphones, accessing through SMS
      messaging attacks 106
Twitter 10, 194
two-factor authentication 86

U

Uniform Commercial Code (UCC)
   about 132, 136
   URL 132
United States Department of Justice
   (US DoJ) 56
United States Federal Bureau of
   Investigation (FBI) 65
updates and compliance 180
URL (Uniform Resource Locator) 195
U.S. Department of Justice 44
users
   personal information, sharing on social
      networking site 11

V

varied password
   creating 97, 98
VentureBeat
   example 70
verbal, extended warranty 135
video chatting 203
Virtual Private Network. *See* **VPN**
viruses
   about 84
   used, for hacking smartphones 9
VPN
   about 169
   using 180
VPN connection
   configuration 169
   IBM Notes Traveler Server, deploying to
      169
VPN technology 166

W

Wall Street Journal (WSJ) 53
warranties, smartphones 129, 134
   As is 131

   cell phone insurance 132, 133
   extended warranty 131, 134
   implied warranty 131
   insurance 134
   lifetime warranty 130, 133
   manufacturer warranty 130, 133
   normal use 131
   standard warranty 133
   utilization 132, 133
weak password 99
Whatsapp 203
Wi-Fi
   using 180
Windows 8 201
Windows Live ID 201
Windows Live PC 201
Windows Mobile 31, 163
Windows Phones 158
Windows RT 171
Windows Server 12 172
Windows Store 201
wireless internet 195
workplace
   mobile devices, using at 63
World Wide Web 195
written statement considerations 136

X

XCode Organizer 91
XML (Extensible Markup Language) 35

Y

Yahoo! 195
young generation
   technology, influences 143, 144
Youtube 194

Z

ZDNet 95
Zeus 84
ZitMo 84

 Thank you for buying
**Mobile Security: How to Secure,
Privatize, and Recover Your Devices**

About Packt Publishing

Packt, pronounced 'packed', published its first book "*Mastering phpMyAdmin for Effective MySQL Management*" in April 2004 and subsequently continued to specialize in publishing highly focused books on specific technologies and solutions.

Our books and publications share the experiences of your fellow IT professionals in adapting and customizing today's systems, applications, and frameworks. Our solution based books give you the knowledge and power to customize the software and technologies you're using to get the job done. Packt books are more specific and less general than the IT books you have seen in the past. Our unique business model allows us to bring you more focused information, giving you more of what you need to know, and less of what you don't.

Packt is a modern, yet unique publishing company, which focuses on producing quality, cutting-edge books for communities of developers, administrators, and newbies alike. For more information, please visit our website: www.packtpub.com.

Writing for Packt

We welcome all inquiries from people who are interested in authoring. Book proposals should be sent to author@packtpub.com. If your book idea is still at an early stage and you would like to discuss it first before writing a formal book proposal, contact us; one of our commissioning editors will get in touch with you.

We're not just looking for published authors; if you have strong technical skills but no writing experience, our experienced editors can help you develop a writing career, or simply get some additional reward for your expertise.

Spring Security 3.1

Secure your web applications from hackers with this
step-by-step guide

Robert Winch
Peter Mularien

Spring Security 3.1

ISBN: 978-1-84951-826-0   Paperback: 456 pages

Secure your web applications from hackers with this
step-by-step guide

1. Learn to leverage the power of Spring Security
   to keep intruders at bay through simple
   examples that illustrate real-world problems

2. Each sample demonstrates key concepts
   allowing you to build your knowledge of the
   architecture in a practical and incremental way

3. Filled with samples that clearly illustrate how to
   integrate with the technologies and frameworks
   of your choice

Oracle 11g Anti-hacker's
Cookbook

Over 50 recipes and scenarios to hack, defend, and secure your
Oracle Database

Foreword by Steven Macaulay, CISSP, OCP, MIS

Adrian Neagu

Oracle 11*g* Anti-hacker's Cookbook

ISBN: 978-1-84968-526-9   Paperback: 302 pages

Over 50 recipes and scenarios to hack, defend, and
secure your Oracle Database

1. Learn to protect your sensitive data by using
   industry certified techniques

2. Implement and use ultimate techniques in
   Oracle Security and new security features
   introduced in Oracle 11*g* R2

3. Implement strong network communication
   security using different encryption solutions
   provided by Oracle Advanced Security

Please check **www.PacktPub.com** for information on our titles

BackTrack – Testing Wireless Network Security

ISBN: 978-1-78216-406-7   Paperback: 108 pages

Secure your wireless networks against attacks, hacks, and intruders with this step-by-step guide

1. Make your wireless networks bulletproof

2. Easily secure your network from intruders

3. See how the hackers do it and learn how to defend yourself

Instant Spring Security Starter

ISBN: 978-1-78216-883-6   Paperback: 70 pages

Learn the fundamentals of web authentication and authorization using Spring Security

1. Learn something new in an Instant!
   A short, fast, focused guide delivering immediate results

2. Learn basic login/password and two-phase authentication

3. Secure access all the way from frontend to backend

4. Learn about the available security models, SPEL, and pragmatic considerations

Please check **www.PacktPub.com** for information on our titles

Lightning Source UK Ltd.
Milton Keynes UK
UKOW06f0328180913

217395UK00002B/37/P